From Chaos to Clarity: The Power of Data Segmentation Explained

Marcel

Contents

CHAPTER 1

Introduction

The book starts sharing the fascination of genome segmentation research in general and the motivation of our multidimensional segmentation algorithms. An overview about the structure of this work is provided, introducing the respective publications.

Data segmentation is the process of segmenting target data according to selected parameters and grouping similar data together so that we can use it more effectively. Segmentation can be done by one- or multi-dimensional segmentation algorithms through simple means, or it can be carried out using sophisticated analytical techniques based on the complexity and dimension of the dataset. Give a data $F:[1,n] \to R\hat{k}$ the segmentation problem consists in finding a partition of the interval $[1,n]$ into subintervals $[a\_i,b\_i]$ such that F is well approximated by a prescribed type of function on each interval $[a\_i,b\_i]$. Multidimensional segmentation is a powerful conceptual model for analyzing large and complex data sets. By subdividing the data set into closely related areas. Multiple and independent segmentations of the whole data set are possible.

Genome segmentation methods are powerful tools for obtaining cell-type or tissue-specific genome-wide annotations and are often used to discover regulatory elements. The segmentation of multivariate time series and -omic data is a common problem in computational biology in general. Over the years, and with increasingly complex measurement procedures, a single data point is usually not just a number or a simple vector, where all components are of the same type. Due to the potential impact of next-generation sequencing NGS, we have seen a rapid increase not only in genomic information but also in annotation information that can be naturally mapped to genomic locations.

Studies in the past decades have shown that genomes usually have a variety of unique and diverse characteristics, all of which together constitute the "blueprint" of organisms. Some of these characteristics are functionally important: promoters, protein-coding sequences, operon, regulatory sequences, etc. Other functions are also important but have evolutionary significance: horizontally transferred regions, prophages, repetitive sequences, etc. In addition, there are other regions of the genome with specific structural characteristics, such as isochores and CpG islands.

In order to determine those functional regions in a genome, it is therefore interesting to determine intervals with coherent function (segments) and find boundaries between them. Many segmentation methods have been developed in recent years; the purpose is to computationally decompose a given genome sequence into parts corresponding to specific structural and functional units.

The change point detection method has been used for genetic data analysis for a long time as an effective tool for studying DNA sequences for various purposes. For example, segmentation methods for categorical variables have been developed to identify patterns of gene prediction [Durot et al., 2009, Braun and Muller].

In the past years, with the widespread use of microarrays, the point-of-change method has been widely used to analyze DNA copy number variations and identify the amplification, mutation or deletion of genomic loci in pathology, such as cancer [Zhang et al., 2012, Erdman and Emerson, 2008], where epigenetic changes are extensively observed in various types of cancer. DNA methylation in the promoter region of a gene can inhibit the expression of cancer-related genes. For example, tumour suppressor may cause carcinogenesis of many cancers, including endometrial cancer [Fiolka et al., 2013, Guida et al., 2009, Kanaya et al., 2003].

The segmentation of multivariate genomic, epigenomic [Karimi et al., 2018], and transcriptomic data from multiple time points, tissue, and cell types to compare changes in genomic organization and to identify common elements form the headline of our research. Next-generation sequencing offers a rich material that can be used in bioinformatics research to find answers, solutions, and exploration for the molecular functions and diseases genetic causes.

Therefore, the main goal of the book project is to design, implement, and test novel segmentation algorithms that work on one- and multidimensional and can accommodate data of different types and resolutions.

Although there are a plethora of segmentation algorithms for genomic features as well as time-series data (reviewed and benchmarked, e.g. in [Braun and Müller, 1998, Elhaik et al., 2010, Girimurugan et al., 2018]), the literature on systematic comparisons of segmentation are comparably sparse.

There are two natural ways to approach this question:

- One class of methods focuses on the breakpoints between segments. Treating them as a signal, significant breakpoints are then detectable as unexpected accumulations across multiple dataset. An example is the C-KS algorithm [Toloşi et al., 2013], which was developed to find consensus breakpoints in cancer genomes.

- An alternative point of view is to consider segmentations of linearly ordered data as partitions of an interval.

Hence (dis)similarity measures for partitions also pertain to segmentation. The problem then can be phrased as finding a segmentation, i.e., a partition of the interval, that is a close as possible to a given collection of segmentations.

The segmentation problem that solves the task of dividing the ordered sequence of data -omic into uniform, approximately constant intervals, has quickly gained practical importance in computational biology, especially on multi-dimensional data tracks.

In our book, we implement 2 Dynamic Programming segmentation algorithms using simulated dataset and experimental dataset. The results showed that the performance of the Jump-sized algorithm and Conseg algorithm are outstanding compared with existing methods. We propose with detailed explanation in the following chapters our two new segmentation algorithms: a new segmentation method, "Jump-sized" based on decomposition threshold and local optimal differentiation, which can detect important breakpoints in the data to identify segmentation boundaries;

The second dynamic algorithm, "Conseg", we derive breakpoint boundaries on the size of consensus segments.

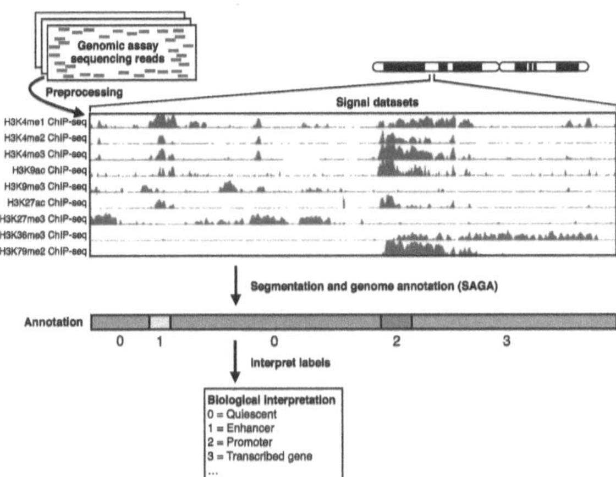

Figure 1.1: ChIP-seq measurements of histone modifications genomic datasets form the input data of segmentation algorithms, which partitions the genome into segments, yielding an annotation and interpretation to assigning a biological interpretation to each segment [Libbrecht et al., 2021]. Figure taken from arXiv:2101.00688v1 [q-bio.GN] 3 Jan 2021.

Figure 1.1 represent the multidimensional segmenation algorithm results of ChIP-seq measurements of histone modifications genomic input dataset, which partitions the genome into segments, yielding an annotation and interpretation to assigning a biological interpretation to each segment.

Structure of this Work

The book starts with a general introduction of biological segmentation algorithms, followed by two chapters introducing the relevant technical and biological concepts.

In chapter 2 (Biological background), basic Bioinformatic methods used in the work context are introduced. In Chapter 3 computational background is briefly summarized, and detailed information of pre-existing segmentation algorithm is provided. Chapter 4 starts with providing the materials and methods used for the segmentation of multivariate data. First, it starts with a general introduction explaining the motivation and target of our implemented algorithm, followed by (1) a methodology describing the detailed steps of the Jump-size algorithm (2) a discussion section to present the segmentation results of simulated data and yeast genome data and (3) conclusion coincide our motivation hypothesis.
Chapter 5 is arranged as follows: Section 2 introduces our algorithm method, describes the algorithm process, and introduces in detail the steps involved in executing the algorithm as well as the generation of simulation data. The third part of the chapter shows and discusses the results of our experiments. Finally, Section 4 summarizes and discusses future research directions.

Finally, Chapter 6 (Conclusion) clearly states a summary of the main achievements as well as an outlook to open questions and future work.

List of Publications

This book is based largely on the following two publications:

[1] **Saker, Halima S.**, Peter F. Stadler, and Ahmad M. Shahin. "Multidimensional segmentation of heterogeneous data." 2017 Fourth International Conference on

Advances in Biomedical Engineering (ICABME). IEEE, 2017.

[2] **Saker, Halima,** Rainer Machné, Jörg Fallmann, Douglas B. Murray, Ahmad M. Shahin, and Peter F. Stadler. "Weighted Consensus Segmentations." Computation 9, no. 2 (2021): 17.

CHAPTER 2

Biological Background

This chapter provides a basic biological background. First outlining the next generation sequencing in general, and then phasing deeper into the topic of data type which is used as input for our sementation algorithm.

2.1 Segmentation of -omic data definition

The genome of an organism is a linear or circular DNA molecule. It can be represented by a symbol string of letters A, T, C and G. At present, the complete genomes
of many organisms are known, which makes it possible to analyze them in detail.
Research in the past decades has shown that genomes usually have various unique
and diverse characteristics, all of which together constitute the "blueprint" of organisms. Some of these characteristics are functionally important such as protein-coding
sequences, regulatory sequences, operators and promoters. In addition, there are
other regions of the genome with specific structural features, such as CpG islands
and isometric axes.

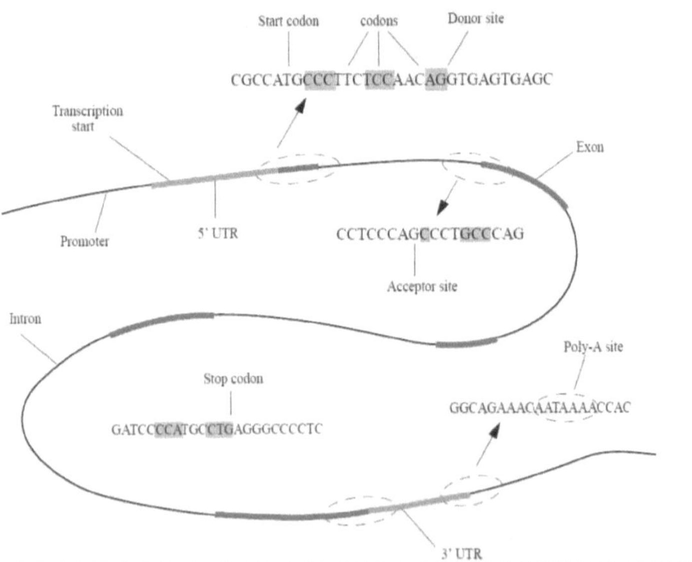

Figure 2.1: *DNA structure with some functional elements are shown.*
Figure taken from Szpankowski, W. et al. (2005). International Journal of Bioinformatics Research and Applications, 1(1), 3-17 [Szpankowski et al., 2005].

A common feature of DNA sequences is that their statistical properties are unevenly distributed along the sequence [Sueoka, 1962]. The typical DNA sequence is non-homogeneous. Therefore, there are contrasts in some areas: rich C+G and poor C+G; protein-coding regions with strong periodic signals are compared with non-coding regions lacking this periodicity, high-density 5′-CG-3′ Dinucleotides (CpG islands) and low-density dinucleotides as showen in Figure 2.1.

The segmentation problem is to find a piece-wise constant approximation to a function defined on one-dimensional independent variables. The function may be, for example, time or genomic coordinates. In the context of detecting changes in copy number in genomic hybridization CGH data and determining transcripts from RNA expression data measured by tiled arrays, this problem appeared as early as the age of genomics. For one-dimensional data segmentation, the coverage can be solved by dynamic programming [Picard et al., 2005]. With the rapid increase in high-throughput data, this problem is commonly used to segment vector-valued data, such as multiple transcriptomes or CGH data from the entire patient population. Once again, a dynamic programming solution can be found [Picard et al., 2011].

Microarray and next-generation sequencing technologies enable researchers to study any genome-wide at the stage of coordination and change. Since biological processes change over time [Yu et al., 2003], it is better to describe them in terms of time-series gene expression rather than static gene expression analysis. To this end, various segmentation methods have been proposed over the last years.

2.2 Next Generation Sequencing

The availability of -Omic data from international companies and global laboratories provides the possibility to answer long-standing questions in biomedicine/molecular biology and to propose new hypotheses for testing. The latest advances in genome sequencing technology have allowed the characterization of various genome features, which has led to the development of several bioinformatics methods that can detect functional elements from next-generation sequencing data. Next-generation sequencing (NGS) is an effective method that scans the entire genome to find DNA copy number changes or modifications (DNA-seq) or transcription regions of the genome (RNA-seq).

Next-generation sequencing (NGS) has made significant strides in sequencing technology; NGS is a new DNA sequencing technology that can sequence millions of bases and genes in a high-throughput manner, in one day and at low cost. This allows many scientists to have access to large biological databases and perform large-scale sequencing [Mardis, 2008].

High-throughput DNA sequencing technology is generating large amounts of data [Korneliussen et al., 2014], therefore, Next-generation sequencing (NGS) platforms can generate large amounts of sequencing data but usually have a high sequencing error rate. For low and medium depth data, fast and effective implementation is needed to process the data, such as segmentation algorithms.
The "big data" obtained by many high-throughput NGS technologies is usually noisy and contains various sources of undesirable differences and artifacts. It is challenging to accurately analyze the amount of unconventional data to identify real signals, combine variable data types and understand the relationship between them [Adli and Bernstein, 2011].

Segmentation algorithms method can process any kind of dense linear signals along the genome. Individual studies have applied segmentation algorithm to DNA replication time series data [Wang et al., 2021, Poulet et al., 2019], interspecies comparative genomics data [Arneson and Ernst, 2019], ChiP-seq data and RNA-seq data [Mendez et al., 2020]. Other studies have even found ways to integrate nonlinear chromatin 3D genomic organization data into the Segmentation algorithms [Libbrecht et al., 2015, Wang et al., 2021]. Nowadays, RNA-seq and ChIP-seq are used frequently to measure gene expression and obtain genome-wide maps of transcription factor, as well as occupancy and epigenetic characteristics [Mahony and Benos, 2007, Livak and Schmittgen, 2001].
NGS generates many kinds of -omic data using different sequencing technologies, such as RNA-seq, CHIP-seq, DNase-seq (deoxyribonuclease-sequencing), ATAC-seq (assay for transposase-accessible chromatin-sequencing) and FAIRE-seq (Formaldehyde-Assisted Identification of Regulatory Elements sequencing).

2.2.1 ChIP-seq

ChIP-Seq technique combines chromatin immunoprecipitation (ChIP) with next-generation sequencing (NGS) to identify genomic sites of DNA-protein binding sites and proposed to use a massive number of cells. Furthermore, ChIP-seq has become the standard technique for identifying locations and biochemical changes. ChIP-seq analysis has become essential for detecting DNA target sites for their corresponding transcription factors (TFs), epigenetic histone modifications, and chromatin remodelling in vivo interactions. The structure and function of chromosomes depend to a large extent on the interaction of nucleic acids with specific proteins [Gilmour and Lis, 1984]. Until now, ChIP-seq is the best technique to study these interactions because of its improved signal-to-noise ratio, and genome sequence information [Song et al., 2016].

2.2.2 RNA-seq

High-throughput Next Generation DNA Sequencing (NGS) technology has revolutionized the field of transcriptomics through enormously parallel sequencing of complementary DNA (cDNA) generated from transcript populations. This critical application of NGS is called RNA sequencing (RNA-seq) [Ozsolak and Milos, 2011]. Considering the importance of sequencing functions, such as throughput, read length, error rate and the ability to perform paired reads, for RNA-seq and genome research, NGS is constantly improving its platform to provide the best sequencing data with the lowest costs sequencing performance. Due to its significant advantages and rapid cost reduction, as well as the application of multiplexing strategies, the RNA-seq method has replaced hybridization-based methods as the preferred method for gene expression research [Salcedo-Amaya et al., 2010]. With the continuous improvement of RNA-seq technology and bioinformatics analysis platform, RNA-seq has been widely used in prokaryotic [Sharma et al., 2010] and eukaryotic [Liu et al., 2015, Ghosh et al., 2015] transcriptome analysis, such as bacterial pathogens, livestock and human cancer and disease research [Tirosh et al., 2016, Guo et al., 2017].

2.3 Main Applications of segmentation in Biology and Biomedecine

2.3.1 Transcriptome Segmentation

Estimating the abundance of messenger RNA transcripts from RNA-Seq data is a crucial task in high-throughput research, which aims to describe the impact of genetic or environmental changes on gene expression. Various methods have solved the combined problem of (gene level) transcription expression quantification and differential alternative RNA processing. Considerable work has been done in this field, dedicated to effective or pseudo-alignment of reads with genome or transcriptome because this is normaly a bottleneck in the analysis process that starts with RNA-Seq reads and generates gene-fragments [Gunady et al., 2018].

Figure 2.2 displays the transcriptome segmentations results obtained with yeast tiling array intensities as data input [Huber et al.].

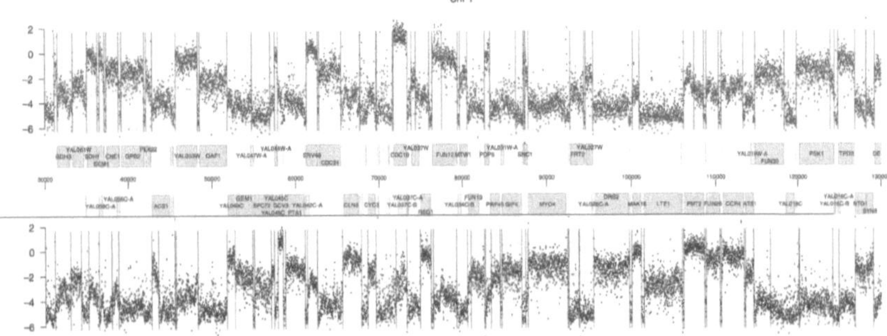

Figure 2.2: Visualization of the array intensity of a yeast slice along chromosome 1 at 100 kb. The figure shows the normalized log2 hybridization intensity (y-axis) along with the genomic coordinates (x-axis of bp). Each point corresponds to a unique probe, the green Watson (+) chain and the blue Crick (-) chain. Annotated open reading frames (ORF) are shown as blue boxes, suspicious ORFs are identified as sky-blue boxes, and transcription factor binding sites are displayed as grey bars. The vertical line is the boundary of the line segment. A method of using data to map the boundaries and levels of all transcripts, including untranslated regions (UTR) of protein-coding genes, antisense transcripts, and currently uncharacterized non-coding RNAs, is described by [David et al., 2006].

2.3.2 Chromatin Segmentation

Chromatin immunoprecipitation followed by sequencing (ChIP-seq) is an increasingly popular experimental method for generating a genome-wide map of histone modifications and analyzing the complexity of the epigenome. Over the last years, many segmentation algorithms were implemented to segment the Chromatin data. Those algorithms have excellent results in the discovering of Tumor and in Cancer researches. An interesting segmentation algorithm, "chromatin-rich", implemented in [Lesack and Naugler, 2012] contribute to the discovering of tumours in nodular tumour subtypes.

Referring to the EpiCSeg method [Mammana and Chung, 2015], which is a segmentation algorithm that combines multiple histone modification maps for segmentation. EpiCSeg provides functional annotations for a significant portion of the genome by using accurate probabilistic models for read counts and shows more robust associations with validation data, and produces more results in repeated experiments and consistent and coherent prediction.

Figure 2.3 shows the main vector output of the EpiCSeg algorithm assigns each genomic bin to one of the states.

2.3.3 Array CGH data segmentation

Array-based Comparative Genome Hybridization (aCGH) is a modern whole-genome measurement technology that can evaluate the occurrence of replication mutations in the entire genome of samples of patients in a reference control genomes, thereby extending the original CGH technology [Masecchia et al., 2013]. Microarray-CGH (Comparative Genome Hybridization) [Gijsbers et al., 2011] experiments are used to detect and locate chromosomal imbalances and irregular and used to scan the entire genome to find changes in DNA copy number. The CGH profile can be viewed as continuous fragments representing homogeneous regions in the genome, and representative sequences of these fragments share the same relative copy number on average [Marioni et al., 2006].

The central task of analyzing aCGH data is to divide probes that share the same DNA copy number into several groups. Some well-known segmentation methods require a long-running time, making interactive data analysis impossible [Willenbrock and Fridlyand, 2005].

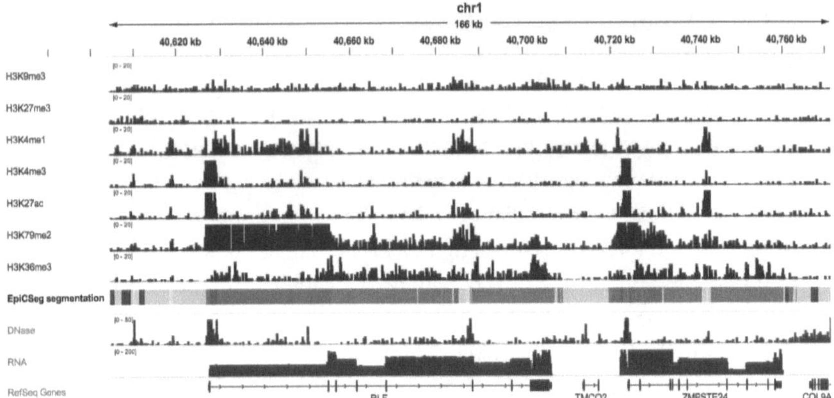

Figure 2.3: EpiCSeg segmentation algorithm result [Mammana and Chung, 2015], the first seven tracks in the top show the input data of EpiCSeg algorithm, which are the read counts for each genomic and for a panel of histone marks. The track number eight represent the result of EpiCSeg segmentation algorithm, it shows the different segment type of chromatine state of the genome, each chromatine is identified by specific color, and the validation data are shown as last three tracks.
Figure taken from Manama & Chung Genome Biology (2015) 16:151 (c) Manama & Chung

Fig 2.4 an example of segmentation results for possible short deletions across four probes is shown. In this example, circular binary segmentation (CBS) is the only method that does not detect the deletion, which shows that CBS is not very sensitive in detecting short fragments and HaarSeg where all the measurements in the same segment share the same value [Ben-Yaacov and Eldar, 2008].

2.3.4 Time Series segmentation

The time-series data from the multi-component system captures the dynamics of the ongoing process and reflects the interaction between the components. For example, in biological systems, these components include genes, proteins, and metabolites, and their changes can be monitored by high-throughput technology [Malone and Oliver, 2011]. In such systems, the progress of the process usually involves checkpoints and events in which the relationships between components change in response to stimuli. Detecting these events together with the components involved can help understand the temporal aspects of complex biological systems. Determined breakpoints are usually associated with significant events leading to component behaviour [Hetland,

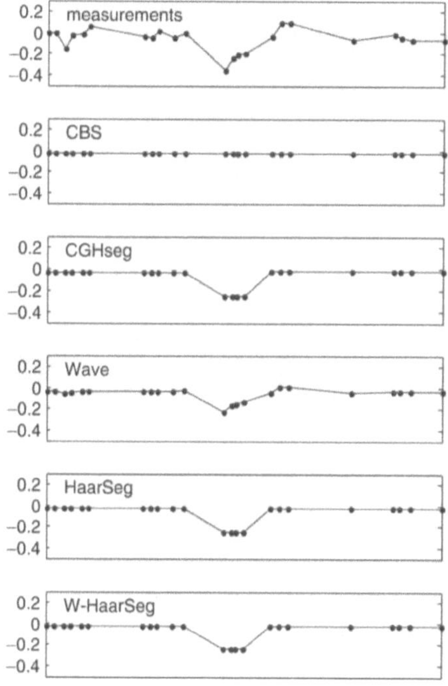

Figure 2.4: present the segmentation results of a possible deletion in chromosome 6, array GSM214509 [Ben-Yaacov and Eldar, 2008].

2004].

However, determining the consensus interval on multiple observed components of a given system is still a challenging computational problem. Multivariate time series segmentation has a wide range of applications in computational systems biology [Omranian et al., 2013], process control [Zou et al., 2011] and market analysis [McCarty and Hastak, 2007].

Figure 2.5 shows the time series segmentation result over yeast's metabolic cycle detailed and cited in [Omranian et al., 2015].

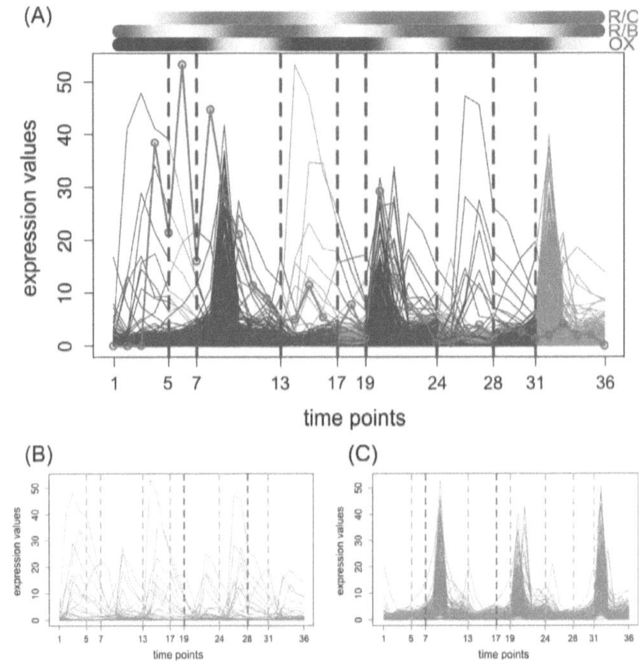

Figure 2.5: result of segmentation over yeast's metabolic cycle from [Omranian et al., 2015]. (A) The expression profile of 255 genes at 36 time points (separated at 25-minute intervals) in three consecutive cell cycles. The green dashed line indicates the breakpoint obtained. According to the biological homogeneity of genes, the genes are divided into two clusters (B) and (C). (B) contains 41 genes and (C) contains 214 genes related to metabolic processes. Each cluster is particularly responsible for the breakpoint indicated by the red dashed line.

CHAPTER 3

Technical Background

This chapter is a technical introduction to segmentation of Multi-variate genome annotation data approaches. Here the tools which were frequently used in this work are presented. The concept of dynamic programming is presented.

As next-generation sequencing data have been included in input data of our studies, the related important segmentation methods and according to analysis are summarized.

In many applications, researchers are not only interested in segmentation, but at the same time, they try to infer clusters of measurements that behave similarly. The model is usually trained by combining Expectation-Maximization (EM) steps, and subsequently, the model is used to generate segments to solve this problem. A mixture of EM and dynamic programming algorithms is used for multi-dimensional CGH data [Picard et al., 2011]. In the context of transcriptomics, a hidden semi-Markov model is used to process the directionality of chain-specific transcriptome data [Du et al., 2014].

A particularly significant version of this problem is chromatin segmentation, which assigns biologically interpretable functional annotations based on histone modification patterns usually measured by ChIP-seq. Then, ChromaSig [Hon et al., 2008] uses a greedy algorithm to expand the seed pattern to determine the fragments. ChromHMM [Ernst and Kellis, 2010], and EpiCSeg are based on Hidden Markov Model (HMM), Segway uses dynamic Bayesian network, and it is recommended to use two-way HMM for binarization (presence/absence) data or ChIP-Seq signal intensity or chromatin Reading counts are modeled for chromatin state. Train the model on a subset of the data, and then use the Viterbi algorithm or its equivalent method to decode the complete data track, that is, to generate segments of the complete dataset.

Segmentation algorithms widely use dynamic programming to calculate the importance of a large number of candidate segments. Next-Generation Sequencing and microarray data [Olshen et al., 2004] form the main input data structure to detect overlapping important areas and update them at the same time. Then, the essential segments are refined, annotated or merged to generate the final segment.

In our book, we implement two Dynamic Programming segmentation algorithms using simulated dataset and experimental dataset, and the results showed that the performance of the Jump-sized algorithm and ConSeg algorithm is outstanding compared with existing methods.

3.1 Dynamic Programming Algorithm

A fundamental approach to solving complex optimization problems is dynamic programming [Yagiura and Ibaraki, 1996] which is an optimization technique. When the optimal solution of the overall problem is composed of the optimal solutions of sub-problems, and these sub-problems usually recur in many different situations, dynamic programming can be used. Dynamic programming is the most essential and basic programming technique in Bioinformatics [Giegerich, 2000] and used widely in Bioinformatics to develop and implement algorithm and pipeline that contribute to analyze and solve the biological problem such as Sequence comparison [Martins et al., 2000, Birney and Durbin, 1997, Delcoigne and Hansen, 1975], gene recognition [Gelfand et al., 1996], RNA structure prediction [Rivas and Eddy, 1999], and hundreds of other problems can be solved by means of dynamic programming [Bussemaker et al., 2000, Li, 2001, Salmenkivi et al., 2002]. Despite all the available experience, applications and algorithm, the development of standard dynamic programming tools is not trivial, and there are many pitfalls in their implementation.

3.2 Dissimilarity measures

The identification of functional elements of the genome usually requires dividing a series of measurements along the genome into segments that are different from adjacent segments. Distance-based clustering and segmentation similarity or dissimilarity (distance) measurement is the core component of the algorithm, and their efficiency directly affects the performance of the clustering algorithm. Hence (dis)similarity measures for partitions, such as the Rand [Rand, 1971], Fowlkes-Mallows [Fowlkes and Mallows, 1983a], Jaccard [Ben-Hur et al., 2002], and Hubert-Arabie [Hubert and Arabie, 1985] indices, or the Mirkin [Mirkin, 1996] and Van Dongen [van Dongen, 2000] metrics also pertain to segmentations. The problem then can be phrased as finding a segmentation, i.e., a partition of the interval, that is as close as possible to a given collection of segmentation.

3.2.1 Rand Index (RI)

RI is a popular quality measure used for the evaluation of time series clustering outcomes resulting from various distance measures, and it is usually used to measure the quality of clustering. It is a measure of the consistency between two groups of objects: the first group is produced by the clustering process, and the other group is defined by external standards and shows how much segmentation results are close to the ground truth. Rand index [Wu et al., 2009] is the most used index for cluster and segments validation [Aghabozorgi et al., 2015, Santos and Embrechts, 2009]. Given X is a finite set with cardinality $|X| = n$, $\mathcal{C} = \{C_1, \ldots, C_k\}$ and $\mathcal{C}' = \{C'_1, \ldots, C'_\ell\}$ two clustering of X, the Rand Index is defined as:

$$\mathcal{R}\left(\mathcal{C},\mathcal{C}'\right) = \frac{2\left(n_{11} + n_{00}\right)}{n(n-1)} \tag{1}$$

where n_{11} is the size of pairs that are in the same cluster under C and C', and n_{00} is the size of pairs that are in different cluster under C and C'

3.2.2 Jaccard

Jaccard similarity index [Jaccard, 1912, Fowlkes and Mallows, 1983b], also known as Tanimoto coefficient, is very similar to Rand Index. This index is applied to measure the similarity of two clusters. It is a ratio of the number of common similarity between the ground truth and the segmented sequence. The Jaccard similarity index is an important indicator to measure the overlap of two sets of data and is excessively used in machine learning, computational genomics, information retrieval and many other fields.

Therefore, the Jaccard is defined as:

$$\mathcal{J}\left(\mathcal{C},\mathcal{C}'\right) = \frac{n_{11}}{n_{11} + n_{10} + n_{01}} \tag{2}$$

Where n_{11} is the size of pairs that are in the same cluster under C and C', and n_{10} is the size of pairs that are in the same cluster under C but in different ones under C' and n_{01} is the size of pairs that are in different clusters under C but in the same under C'.

3.2.3 Hubert-Arabie

Called also Adjusted Rand Index (ARI): the adjusted Rand index is the standardized difference between the Rand index and its expected value under the null (zero) hypothesis. Hubert and Arabie proposed an adjustment that assumes the null hypothesis of the generalized distribution: these two clusters are drawn randomly, with a fixed number of clusters and a fixed number of elements in each cluster. ARI is more effective than RI and many other indices. This method has been successfully used in gene expression domains [Yeung et al., 2001a,b].

Therefore, the Hubert-Arabie Index is defined as:

$$\mathcal{R}_{adj}\left(\mathcal{C},\mathcal{C}'\right) = \frac{\sum_{i=1}^{k}\sum_{j=1}^{\ell}\binom{m_{ij}}{2}-t_3}{\frac{1}{2}(t_1+t_2)-t_3}$$

$$\text{where } t_1 = \sum_{i=1}^{k}\binom{|C_i|}{2}, t_2 = \sum_{j=1}^{\ell}\binom{|C_j'|}{2}, t_3 = \frac{2t_1t_2}{n(n-1)} \tag{3}$$

Where m_{ij} is the *confusion matrix* M or contingency table of the pair C, C':

$$m_{ij} = \left|C_i \cap C_j'\right|$$

3.2.4   Mirkin Metric

Known as Equivalence Mismatch Distance. If the set of all element pairs is enumerated, and the cluster is represented by the binary vector defined in this enumeration, it corresponds to the Hamming distance of the binary vector. However, Mirkin Metric is very sensitive to the cluster size, so two clusters "at right angles" to each other are closer to each other than two clusters when one cluster is an improvement of the other cluster. The Mirkin metric system is a variant of the Rand index and can be defined as:

$$\mathcal{M}\left(\mathcal{C},\mathcal{C}'\right) = 2\left(n_{01} + n_{10}\right) = n(n-1)\left(1 - \mathcal{R}\left(\mathcal{C},\mathcal{C}'\right)\right) \tag{4}$$

3.3   Segmentation Algorithms

In this book, we propose a new algorithm to capture the consensus of information from a set of segmentations generated by varying parameters of different algorithms. We achieve this goal by determining consensus partitions from a heterogeneous set of hypothetical segmentation.

Since no effective methods exist for choosing optimal parameters in multidimensional segmentation, there is also a growing interest to combine several segmentations obtained using different parameter settings or different segmentation algorithms into a final consensus segmentation.

In this section we briefly overview some pre-existing genomic segmentation approaches based on supervised and unsupervised methods to investigate the use of those proposed segmentation approach results as input data for our proposed consensus segmentation Conseg.

The number of segmentation method used has increased recently due to the wide availability of genomics dataset, such as Chromatin colors [Filion et al., 2010], Chromatin states model [Ernst and Kellis, 2010], iSeg [Zacher et al., 2017] and Spectacle [Song and Chen, 2015].

Segmentation algorithms are widely used to understand genome activity and gene regulation. These algorithms use -omic data, genomic, epigenomic [Kundaje et al., 2015], transcriptomic and proteomic dataset as input [Zitnik et al., 2019], such as histone modifications , RNA-Seq data [Cleynen et al., 2014a], gene expression data, aCGH data or chromatin immunoprecipitation sequencing (ChIP-seq) measurements.

3.3.1   k-segmetation algorithm according to Bellmann

Richard Bellman may be known for his most significant contribution to algorithms, and that is the development of dynamic programming.

The standard dynamic programming algorithm can optimize the solution of the K-segmentation problem generated by Bellman.

Given a sequence T of length n and a value k, find a k contiguous segmentation $S = \{s_1, s_2, \ldots, s_k\}$ of T such that and the E_p error is minimized, and μ_s the representative of the segment.

$$E_p(S) = \left(\sum_{s \in S} \sum_{t \in s} |t - \mu_s|^p \right)^{\frac{1}{p}} \tag{5}$$

$$\mu_S = \frac{1}{|s|} \sum_{t \in s} t \tag{6}$$

Cases for the error function E_p:

$p = 1$, the best μ_s corresponds the median of the points in segment s.

$p = 2$, the best μ_s corresponds to the mean of the points in segment s. The dynamic programming of the K-segmentation method uses dynamic programming recursion to extend the solution of smaller size problem and stores the solutions to the sub-problems using the DP table [DPt].

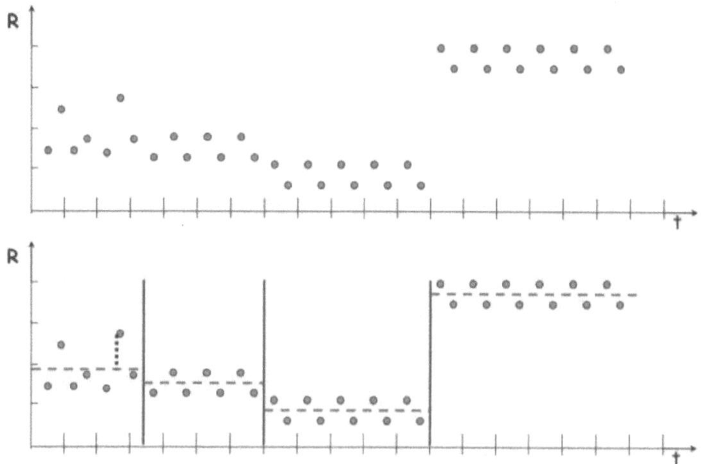

Figure 3.1: K-segmentation example

3.3.2 SegRNA segmentation algorithm

SegRNA can identify repetitive signal combinations across multiple dataset to measure the abundance of transcribed RNA. SegRNA is an unsupervised method that allows exploration of data patterns without relying on the existing record model and takes as input multi-, and diverse transcriptomic dataset from any cell type [Mendez et al., 2020]. SegRNA uses multiple transcriptome dataset to generate simple annotations. These annotations allow biologists to quickly examine hypotheses about transcription patterns across the genome. As we show here, SegRNA annotations can be used as building blocks, and combining them together can simplify transcriptome multiple dimensional dataset.

3.3.3 Hidden Markov model

The most common segmentation method of -omic data is an instance of Hidden Markov Model (HMM), which is a probabilistic model of the relationship between the sequence of observation events and the unobservable hidden state that generates the observation event. The structure of HMM naturally reflects the segmentation algorithm task, which is to cluster observed data generated by the processes focusing on the sequence of genomic positions. Hidden Markov model is used to model the count matrix and obtain segmentation (ex. ChromHMM).

ChromHMM

Chromatin state annotation combined with chromatin modification patterns has become a powerful method for discovering specific activity patterns of regulatory regions and their cell types, and for interpreting disease-related research [Day et al., Ernst and Kellis, 2012, Ernst and Kellis, Filion et al., 2010, Roy et al., 2010]. ChromHMM is an automated computing system for learning chromatin state, characterizing its biological function and relevance to large-scale functional dataset, and visualizing the entire chromatin state to annotate whole-genome maps. ChromHMM is based on a multivariate hidden Markov model HMM, which uses the product of independent Bernoulli random variables to model the observed combination of chromatin markers, which can reliably learn many complex patterns of chromatin modification.

TreeHMM

Tree hidden Markov model (TreeHMM) [Biesinger et al., 2013] is a graphical segmentation algorithm used to discover and map chromatin states using the observed epigenetic chromatin modification data and based on measurements from different cell types in a principled way. TreeHMM is implemented in combination with junction tree algorithm [Dean and Kanazawa, 1988] and Graphical Models Toolkit (GMTK) [Bilmes and Bartels, 2012]. TreeHMM can incorporate tag information that is only available in a certain cell types and adapt to more interesting tree structures by including other potential cell types.

hiHMM

A new Bayesian non-parametric method, called Hierarchical Linked Infinite HMM (hiHMM) [Sohn et al., 2015], can use genome-wide histone modification data to jointly infer staining in multiple genomes (different species, cell types, and developmental stages) Qualitative state diagram. This flexible framework provides a new way to learn a consistent definition of chromatin state across multiple genomes, thereby facilitating direct comparison between them. hiHMM has many application in the human/Drosophila/worm cross-species shows the chromatin state segmentation in a single organism.

diHMM

Hierarchical hidden Markov model (diHMM) is a new computational method developed to annotate systematically at multiple length scales the chromatin states [Marco et al., 2017]. diHMM can accurately capture the nucleosome level information and identify the domain-level state that changes in the nucleosome level state composition, spatial distribution, and function. The status at the domain level summarizes known patterns such as super-enhancers, bivalent promoters, and Polycomb inhibitory regions and identifies other patterns that have not yet characterized their biological functions. By integrating chromatin status information with gene expression, diHMM determined the context-related functions of nucleosome-level status. diHMM provides a powerful tool for studying the role of higher-order chromatin structure in gene regulation.

modHMM

ModHMM is a new HMM-based modular segmentation method. ModHMM segmentation shows a better balance between accuracy and recall. The classifier associated with each hidden state of ModHMM can detect a well-defined chromatin state. ModHMM algorithm leads to segmentation with advantages in terms of quality. Functional elements, such as active enhancers or promoters, are usually contained in a single segment element [Benner and Vingron, 2020]. Therefore, ModHMM is a relevant alternative for studying epigenetics and within cells type or tissues.

ConsHMM

ConsHMM [Arneson and Ernst, 2019] method is used to assign a conservative state to each nucleotide in the human genome. These states capture the unique enrichment of other genome annotations, such as gene annotations, CpG islands, repeat families, chromatin status, genetic variation, and bases prioritized by variant priority scoring. ConsHMM protection status annotation is a resource for explaining genome and potential disease-related variants, complementing existing protection and epigenome-based annotations.

EpiCSeg

Epigenome Count-based Segmentation (EpiCSeg) [Mammana and Chung, 2015] is a segmentation algorithm that use accurate discrete multivariate probability distributions to model the count vector of a given hidden state, which can summarize the over-dispersion and related features observed in the data besides the probability framework and calculation efficiency and can also be used for large genomes, such as the human genome. The main function of EpiCSeg is to perform multivariate modeling of read-counts from multiple histone markers and then integrate it into a Hidden Markov Model **(HMM)** to generate fragments of the genome.

3.3.4 Segway

Segway method uses Dynamic Bayesian Networks DBN technology to segment and cluster genomic data such as human chromatin immunoprecipitation sequencing (ChIP-seq), DNase-seq, FAIRE-seq data Application [Hoffman et al., 2012, Chan et al., 2018, Libbrecht et al., 2019]. Segway models the emission parameters with a multivariate Gaussian distribution. In an unsupervised manner, we determined patterns related to the transcription start sites, gene ends, enhancers, transcription regulator CTCF binding regions and repressor regions.

3.3.5 Bayesian Approach

The Bayesian segmentation method was used previously [Booth and Smith, 1982, Liu and Lawrence, 1999] describing a general Bayesian method that can find the changing points distribution along the sequence, that is, the potential possibility is a polynomial. Through calculations, they use dynamic programming methods to accelerate Bayesian analysis. Further applications for DNA segmentation in the Bayesian technique are given in [Ramensky et al., 2000].

CHAPTER 4

Multidimensional Segmentation of Heterogeneous Data

High-throughput methods are generating more and more omics data - such as genomic, proteomic, transcriptomic data- that provide more and more detailed and rich genome annotations. Combining these data into regions with consistent behavior is the core of functional genome annotation work. The segmentation problem that solves the task of dividing the ordered sequence of data -omic into uniform, approximately constant intervals, has quickly gained a practical importance in computational biology, especially on multi-dimensional data tracks. We propose in the following chapter a new segmentation method based on decomposition threshold and local optimal differentiation, which can detect important break points in the data to identify segmentation boundaries.

4.1 Introduction

In general, modern -omics dataset are composed of multiples types of data and often also replicates and/or data of the same type from different biological conditions. Therefore, the segmentation problem has to solved in a manner that integrates this multitude of data tracks [Keogh et al., 2001, Guéguen, 2005, Huber et al., 2006, Badagián et al., 2015].

There are two fundamentally different methods to solve this segmentation problem:

- Multidimensional data can be segmented as a unit [Boys and Henderson, 2004, Terzi and Tsaparas, 2006, Bingham, 2010, Machné et al., 2017], like the usual methods in chromatin segmentation.

- Alternatively, each data track can be split independently; then the interval end time must be coordinated in a second independent step.

In this contribution, we will adopt the second method, which is the first investigation that discusses effective methods for segmenting time-series dataset or whole-genome dataset.

A common problem with segmentation methods is the difference between random variation/noise and the true boundaries of segment. Generally, a measure of acceptable variability within a segment or the expected number of segments is provided as a user-defined input parameter. Instead, we consider the observed jump size distribution here to estimate the important step size directly from the data. The proposed method was evaluated with the help of simulated data with different noise levels and relative intensities. Since our method first divides each time series data track into multiple segments, it can adapt to different noise levels and related attributes, because the data adaptive segmentation is performed independently for each data dimension.

The content of this chapter is arranged as follows: Section 2 introduces our algorithm method, describes the algorithm process, and introduces in detail the steps involved in the execution of the algorithm and the generation of simulation data. The third part of the chapter shows and discusses the results of our experiments. Finally, Section 4 summarizes and discusses future research directions.

4.2 Methodology

4.2.1 Algorithm process

Figure 4.1 shows a flowchart summarizing the steps involved in our algorithm.

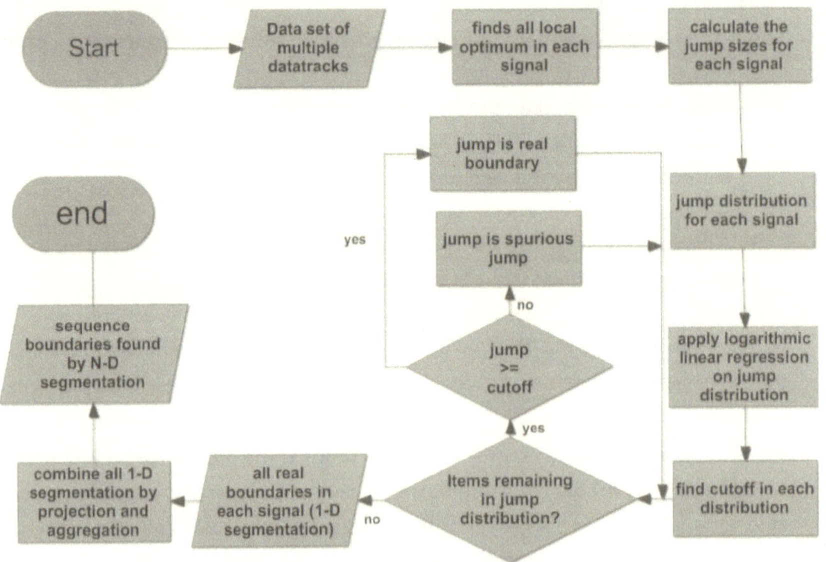

Figure 4.1: A flowchart summarizing the steps of Jump-size algorithm

After all the local optima in each data track signal are found [Boriah, 2010], the "jump sizes" will be calculated, that is, the signal difference between successive local optima. From these values, the jump size distribution shown in the figure 4.2 is extracted. The size of jumps that occur at high frequencies is considered noise, while the size of jumps observed at low frequencies may be the true segment boundaries.

We observe that the size of frequent jumps at least follows the exponential distribution in Figure 4.2. Therefore, we can use linear regression (log-transformed data) to estimate the size of the jump that is expected to be observed only once in the data, thereby determining the natural threshold of the effective jump size. In future

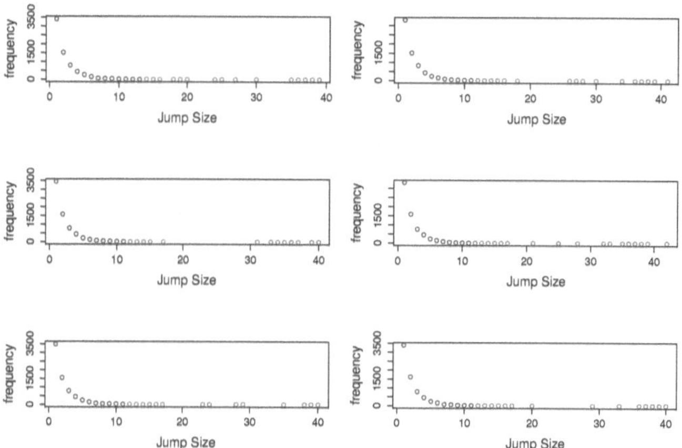

Figure 4.2: Jump size distribution of 6 synthetic data dimensions The simulated sample dataset used throughout the contribution process. The data points marked in red correspond to known segment boundaries.

work, this simple heuristic method should be replaced by a more complex jump size distribution estimation. Since each data track is considered separately, the cut-off value of each data dimension is estimated independently, see Figure 4.3.

The Cut-point is regarded as the intersection between the two linear regression lines. All points exist before the Cut-point are considered as noise jumps, and all points exist after the Cut-point are considered as actual jumps that can be divided into line segment boundaries. The effective transition points of each data track are combined into the multi-dimensional segment boundary. In order to prove the applicability and feasibility of our method, we use a simple majority voting procedure. If a minimum number of valid jumps are found within a user-defined interval with a small width, then a single segment boundary is called. In the future, this simple heuristic method will need to replace the positioning accuracy of jumping points in each data track with statistically reasonable estimates. Throughout the use of this contribution,the simulated dataset includes 15228 individual points, 20 segments with data values uniformly sampled from normal distribution, and a superimposed Gaussian noise with different standard deviations ratio (0.5, 0.8, and 1.0).

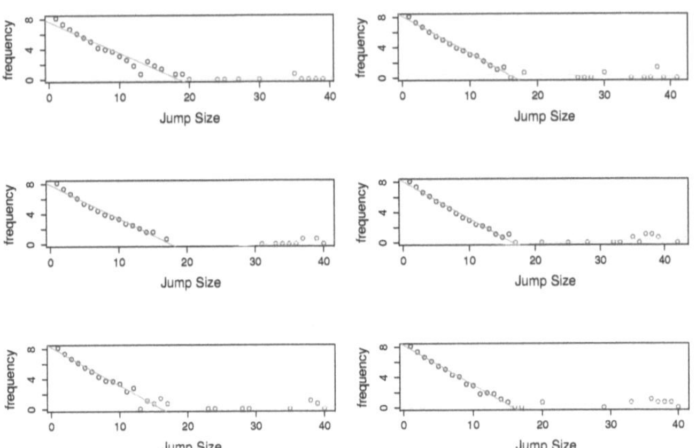

Figure 4.3: The logarithmic representation of the jump size distribution highlights the approximate exponential distribution of noise jumps, and a simple regression method is proposed to determine the boundary between true jumps and false jumps.

4.2.2 Data generation

In order to study the function of this method, we designed an artificial benchmark dataset in order to know the ground truth in advance (that is, the position of the jump in each data dimension) is called *a priori*. Artificial data is generated by dividing the "genome" into intervals of randomly selected lengths. Correlate different data tracks by generating an average value for the data track and each interval. These values are randomly selected again to obtain a a i.i.d. uniform distribution. Therefore, the ideal signal is a function of the sequence position that is constant in each interval. However, real data such as gene expression data sometimes suffer from large measurement errors. To model this contribution, noise is added to each DNA location [Zhang et al., 2008]. For simplicity, we use i.i.d. noise drawing here to form a Gaussian distribution with prescribed variance. In order to study the effect of correlation in noise, we used the smoothing method of running average.We generate artificial data with different Gaussian noise levels, as shown in Figure 4.4.

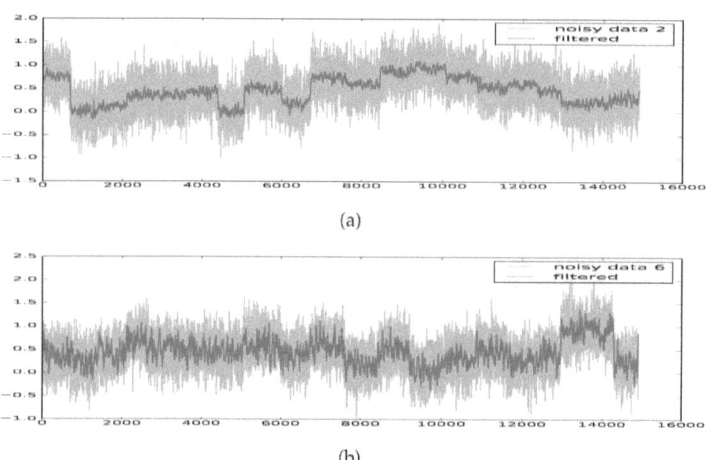

(a)

(b)

Figure 4.4: Examples of synthetic simulated data (intensity) with different ratio of Gaussian noise using different standard deviation scales ((a) 0.5 and (b) 0.8) superimposed on the same ideal segmentation data.

4.3 Segmentation of Simulated Data

From the simulated data-set, the 1-dimensional segmentation algorithm summarized in the past section is utilized to readily recognize the segmentation break points of every data-track. An Example is shown from the figure 4.5

The aggregation of one-dimensional boundaries leads to the desired multi-dimensional segmentation. In our simulation data, we have observed excellent representation of the original segment boundaries, see Figure 4.6. Based on experience, we have observed that the accuracy of segmentation increases as the dimensionality of the data increases.

The target data of this work is multivariate genetic/epigenetic data. The reason is that these datasets can change under the influence of a variety of conditions, such as chemical, genetic, and epigenetic modifications. For this reason, under all these conditions and in genetic/epigenetic variation [Van der Sluis et al., 2015], the signal required for real data is a function of coverage and expression values. The simplest sub-problem in segmentation is to determine whether two adjacent intervals should

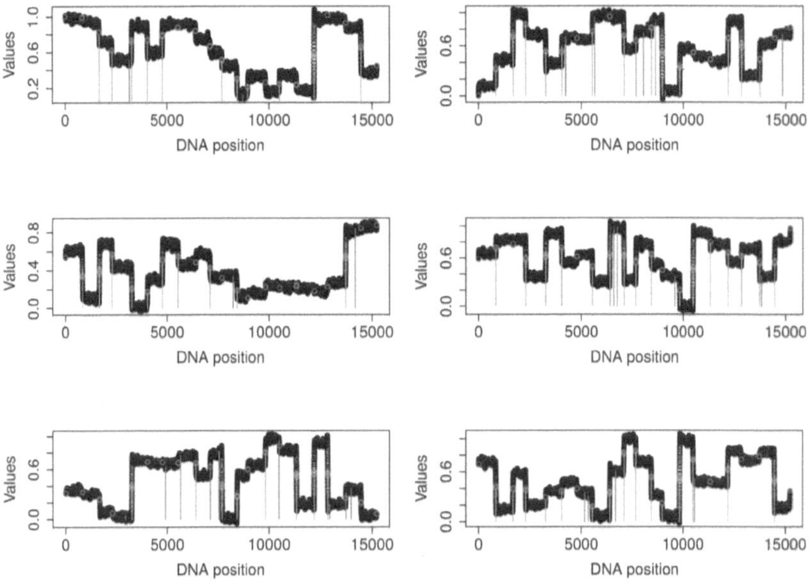

Figure 4.5: The result of independent one-dimensional segmentation of our synthetic data of six data dimensions. on X-axis are DNA coordinate, and on Y-axis are the artificial intensity values. The green lines indicate jumps called segment boundaries. Note that not all segment boundaries are identified in each individual dimension. The red line represents the false alarm boundary.

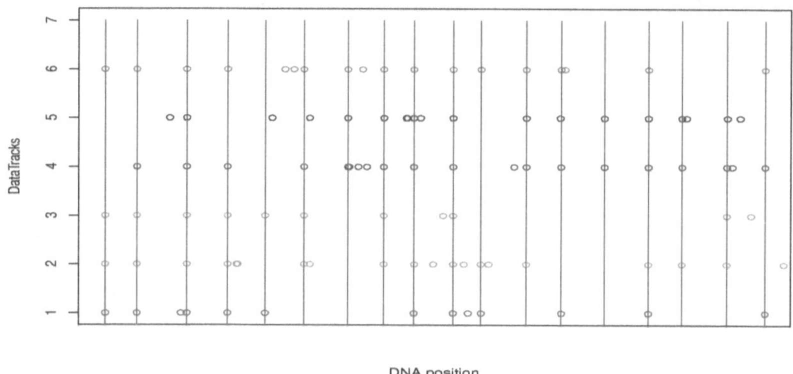

Figure 4.6: Combine the determined one-dimensional segmentation boundaries of my artificial data with multi-dimensional data segmentation process. The vertical lines are the boundaries determined by my N-D algorithm, and they match the expected results in the simulated data.

form two different segments, or should they be combined into a single segment. We have to figure out what to do in multidimensional segmentation; in 1-D, this is well known. The problem of global segmentation can then be viewed as making local decisions in a consistent manner. By identifying the possible segmentation boundaries in each data dimension, the pursued method can be regarded as a candidate for generating multi-dimensional segmentation. In addition to summarizing the boundaries, statistical tests that consider the importance of multi-dimensional jumps at such candidate positions may also be fruitful.

4.4 Segmentation of yeast transcriptome data

We addressed the problem of multidimensional segmentation of heterogeneous data, we applied the therein developed algorithm to *Sacchromyces cerevisiae* dataset. As expected many more parameters need to be taken into account when applying an approach not only to artificial data but also to a real world problem. We use a conceptually simple scheme for segmenting multi-dimensional transcriptomic data, implementing an algorithm for identifying sequence boundaries and the manipulation of those boundaries once identified. The goal is to detect significant breakpoints for each data track, and then aggregate the 1-D segmentation to identify segment boundaries. Our preliminary results, summarized in Figure 4.8, clearly indicate an improvement of the predicted segmentation when compared to existing annotation approach!

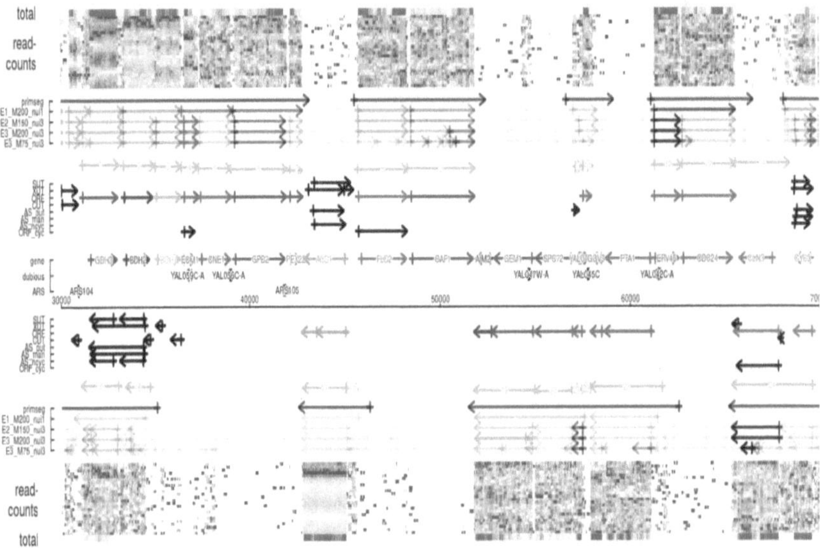

Figure 4.7: *A densely transcribed example Domain of* S. cerevisiae's *chromosome I (chrI:300000 . . . 50000) is shown. The solid black line in the middle separates the forward and reverse strand data. Directly above and below that line the corresponding given annotation is shown as a gold standard. Gray arrows highlight the segmentation resulting from our approach while colored arrows named E1-E3 represent the output of SegmenTier. This figure represents an extended version of Figure 4 in the SegmenTier publication* [Machné and Stadler, 2020].

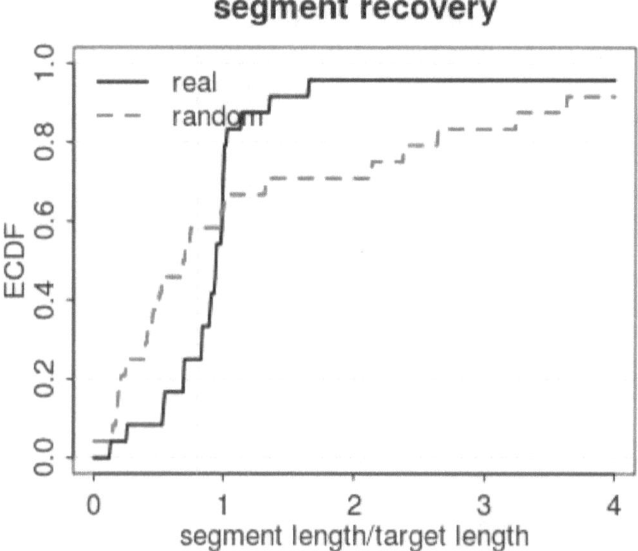

Figure 4.8: A segment recovery test plotting the empirical cumulative distribution function (ECDF) of S. cerevisiae *segmentation shows the superiority of our approach (solid line) over the SegmenTier algorithm (dashed line).*

4.5 Concluding Remarks

Here we propose a conceptually simple scheme for segmenting multi-dimensional data on linearly ordered domains. Using simulated data, we proved that the jump size distribution can be used to determine important interval boundaries in a data-adaptive manner independent of each data dimension. These segment boundaries can then be combined into multi-dimensional segments. Here, we used a simple voting procedure to merge the important jumps in a sufficiently close distance of each data track. This work is only the first step. Several issues have been identified, and we hope that major improvements can be made in the future: First, a better jump size distribution model will allow a better, statistically reasonable cut-off value –although simple regression heuristics have worked, at least in simulations The data is very good. Second, the current rules for combining the segment boundaries of each data track involve a width parameter, which should also be estimated from the data. Our framework can accommodate different types of data, such as genetics, epigenetics, proteomics and transcriptomics data. It is particularly valuable to combine data with different accuracy and resolution. Since the boundaries of each data track are estimated independently, the aggregation process is expected to identify multi-dimensional segmentation with a resolution comparable to that of the best resolution of a single data track.

CHAPTER 5

Weighted Consensus Segmentations

The problem of segmentation of linear data is often encountered in time series analysis, computational biology and natural language processing. Segmentation obtained independently from the same data by copying dataset or using different methods or parameter settings brings about the problem of computational aggregation or consensus segmentation. This SEGMENTATION AGGREGATION problem is equivalent to finding a segment that minimizes the sum of the input segment distances. This is another segmentation problem, which can be solved by dynamic programming. The purpose of this contribution is:

1. to gain a better mathematical understanding of SEGMENTATION AGGREGATION problems and their solutions and applications.

2. to prove that consensus segmentation has useful applications.

Extending previously known segmentation boundaries results we show that for a large class of distance functions only breakpoints present in at least one input segmentation appear in the consensus segmentation. Furthermore, we derive a break point boundaries on the size of consensus segments. As show-case applications we investigate a yeast transcriptome and show that consensus segments provide a robust means of identifying transcriptomic units. This approach is in particularly suited for dense transcriptomes with polycistronic transcripts, or a lack of separation between transcripts and operons. As a second application we demonstrate that consensus segmentations can be used to robustly identify growth plan from sets of replicate growth curves.

5.1 Introduction

In computational biology, the problem of one-dimensional segmentation appears in the analysis of microarray and high-throughput DNA or RNA sequencing data. Segmentations obtained independently from replicates of experiments or from the same data by applying different segmentation methods or different parameter settings in the same segmentation method bring about the problem of computing a consensus result, please refer to [Pirooznia et al., 2015].

In epigenomics, the frequent pattern of histone modification defines genomic intervals that can be associated with functional units including gene bodies, enhancers or promoters. See, for example, [Yen and Kellis, 2015] and references therein. One of segmentation problem is the identification of transcription units, including distinguishing between expressed and unexpressed loci [Zeller et al., 2008, Hardcastle et al., 2012] or operon [Bischler et al., 2014], or more commonly, to distinguish adjacent or even the advantage of no unexpressed spacer between overlapping transcripts.

Those tasks are particularly relevant for organisms with "compact" genomes, such as bacteria [Bischler et al., 2014] or yeast [David et al., 2006, Danford et al., 2011], in which transcribed loci are hardly separated into non expressed regions. The boundary between transcriptional segment can be detected by the difference in RNA levels [David et al., 2006], see for example SRG1 ncRNA in Fig. 5.1. For example, [Braun and Müller, 1998, Elhaik et al., 2010, Girimurugan et al., 2018] provides many segmentation algorithms for genome features and time series data, and benchmarks them.

In each data track, the boundaries between segments are usually not clearly visible. This type of limitation can often be moderated by aggregating many experiments or measurements. For example, in the yeast RNA-seq data shown in Fig. 5.1, transcriptome samples at different time points in the respiratory cycle are aggregated, and the signal information generated is much important than the level of a RNA expression level at single Point in time. Nevertheless, any specific parameter selection (here, the selection of the similarity measure of the temporal coverage profiles of adjacent nucleotides) will produce false positive and false negative segment boundaries.

Fig. 5.1 indicates that improvements can be achieved by aggregating different segments into a single consensus. In a similar way , [Hardcastle et al., 2012] uses simple

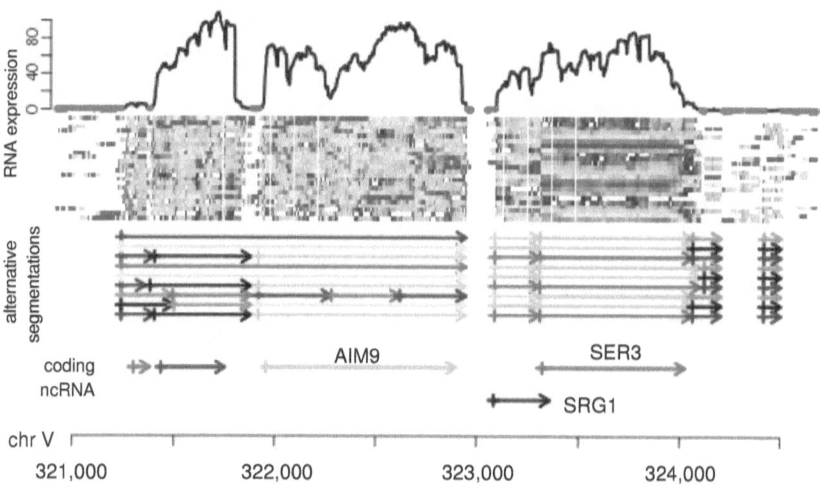

Figure 5.1:
Segmentation of RNA expression patterns. Above: RNA expression in 24 samples collected from Saccharomyces cerevisae IFO 0233 strain every 4 minutes (shown by color scale, the total number of all experiments above). The sequencing data is strand-specific, showing only the positive strand of about 5,000 nt on the V chromosome. Medium: Use segmenTier to calculate nine different segmentations using different parameter settings. For details on data and segmentations, please refer to [Machné et al., 2017]. Bottom: Annotated coding and non-coding yeast genes. The short segment at the far right is a candidate site for the unannotated ncRNA, which is anti-sense to the longer protein-coding gene Utp7p on the negative strand. The data is the same as Fig. 3 of [Machné et al., 2017].

heuristic segmentation to detect candidate loci, uses them as intervals, and is scored by the statistical model of each RNA-seq experiment, and then uses the problem-specific greedy heuristic to determine the consensus interval boundary is used for the expression of ncRNA locus. The segmentation method of bacterial RNA-seq data in [Bischler et al., 2014] return the optimal segmentation of sequence with different numbers of K segments, and uses a voting procedure to reach a consensus on the different values of K. These examples raise an important inquiry of whether there is a more principled aggregation segmentation method in a single consensus segmentation.

Figure 5.2 displays the segmentations results obtained with five segmentation methods for gene YAL030W [Cleynen et al., 2014b]

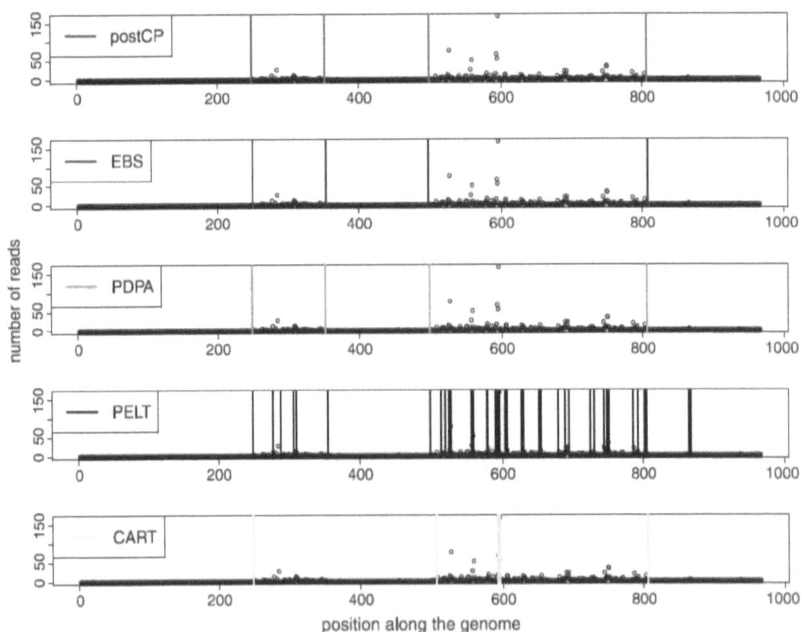

Figure 5.2: Segmentation results of gene YAL030W from five different segmentation methods, segmentation is based on actual RNA-Seq read counts [Cleynen et al., 2014b].

This problem also appears in a more general context. Modern *omics research usually reports its results in the form of genome browser tracks, that is, the reference genome is segmented into intervals. The comparison and merging of these data naturally requires consensus or reference. This is especially true for annotations based on epigenome or transcriptome data. Here, there is a great need for an effective method in principle to compare annotations that exceed quantitative overlap, so as to avoid a complete re-analysis of the basic raw data. In contrast to genome browser tracks, raw data usually requires a lot of processing and is not directly accessible under any circumstances. Although consensus segmentation has obvious potential uses, the literature on systematic comparison of segmentation is very sparse. Two natural ways to solve this problem have been considered:

(i) focuses on the break-points between segments, and use them as signals. Then, through the C-KS algorithm[Toloşi et al., 2013], important (consensus) breakpoints can be detected as an accumulation among multiple datasets. More generally, this can be seen as a breakpoints clustering problem [Segal and Wiemels, 2002].

(ii) The segments of linearly sorted data form sequence partitions. Dissimilarity measures of partitions, such as the Rand [Rand, 1971], Fowlkes-Mallows [Fowlkes and Mallows, 1983a], Jaccard [Ben-Hur et al., 2002], and Hubert-Arabie [Hubert and Arabie, 1985] indices, or the Mirkin [Mirkin, 1996] and Van Dongen [van Dongen, 2000] metrics are also suitable for special cases of segmentation. The MEDIAN PARTITIONING problem, also called consensus clustering problem, is to find a partition as close as possible to the given set w.r.t. for these dissimilarity measures [Mirkin, 1975, Barthélemy and Leclerc, 1995]. MEDIAN PARTITION is NP complete [Křivánek and Morávek, 1986, Wakabayashi, 1998]. It is in this second method that we further pursue this contribution.

The SEGMENTATION AGGREGATION problem [Mielikäinen et al., 2006] is a specialization of the partition of linear ordered sets (such as time series or genome sequences): given a collection of m one dimensional segmentations $S_1, S_2, \ldots, S_m$ on the interval, and the distance function D between input segmentations, the task is to find the segment C make Minimize the sum of distances

$$f(\mathbf{C}) := \sum_{q=1}^{m} D(\mathbf{C}, \mathbf{S}_q).\tag{1}$$

We assume that $D(.,.)$ is a dissimilarity, i.e., that (i) $D(\mathbf{S}, \mathbf{S}') \geq 0$, and (ii) $D(\mathbf{S}, \mathbf{S}') = 0$ if $D(\mathbf{S} = \mathbf{S}'$. In most cases $D(.,.)$ will be a metric. However, neither symmetry nor triangle inequality is necessary. As shown in [Mielikäinen et al., 2006], compared with MEDIAN PARTITION under normal circumstances, SEGMENTATION AGGREGATION can accurately solve some interesting distance metrics through dynamic programming, including divergence or Mirkin metric and Information distance. Mailă [Meilă, 2005] uses an axiomatic method based on certain additivity conditions in the partition to show that "variation of information" [Meilă, 2003], that is, information distance [Mielikäinen et al., 2006] is essentially the only natural distance between segments. However, we have considered a wider range of difference measures here. Despite its attractive features, that is, there are almost no model assumptions and no detailed knowledge of the input segmentation source is required, but SEGMENTATION AGGREGATION is rarely used in actual data analysis. Here, we prove that this is a useful and effective segmentation method.

A given set of input data is often affected by bias, such as the uneven distribution of taxa in comparative genomics, or the uneven distribution of samples between treatment groups. In order to reach a consensus approach, it is usually necessary to keep all data. As a remedy for sampling bias, many weighting schemes have been proposed to correct the bias by assigning greater weight to under-represented data and assigning less weight to overrepresented data. For comparison, see [Vingron and Sibbald, 1993]. In the case of segmentation of genome features or time series, for example, due to the different levels of noise in each data track, the trust degree in each individual segmentations $\mathbf{S}_q$ may be different. It may also be necessary to process biological copies other than technical copies. Naturally, this difference can be expressed by introducing a segment-specific weight w_q. As we will see below, this weight can be introduced directly in SEGMENTATION AGGREGATION.

In this chapter, we studied a weighted version of the segmentation aggregation problem, aiming to gain insight into the properties of consensus segmentation. Particularly, we summarized the previous results of consensus breakpoints boundaries, and obtained the upper limit of the consensus segment length of a large class of distance functions. Then, we consider two important applications of consensus segmentation:

using the yeast transcriptome as a display example to identify the transcriptional units, and segmentation of microbial growth curves. At the end, we will briefly discuss some open questions about the theory behind consensus segmentation and its practical application.

5.2 Theory

5.2.1 Dynamic Programming Algorithm

The WEIGHTED SEGMENTATION AGGREGATION approach is a moderate generalization of the unweighted version considered in [Mielikäinen et al., 2006].We shall see that properties of the unweighted problem and its solution generalize to the weighted version. Given a set of $\{S_q | 1 \leq q \leq m\}$ input segmentation and corresponding weight $w_q > 0$ to quantify the relative importance of contribution segmentation S_q, the task is to minimize the objective function

$$f(\mathbf{C}) := \sum_{q=1}^{m} w_q D(\mathbf{C}, \mathbf{S}_q) \,, \tag{2}$$

i.e., the weighted total dis-similarity of the unknown consensus segmentation $\mathbf{C}$. Without losing generality, we can assume $\sum_{q=1}^{m} w_q = 1$.

Referring to [Mielikäinen et al., 2006], we defined a distance metric D, which can be represented in terms of the *common refinement* $\mathbf{S}' \wedge \mathbf{S}'' := \{A \cap B | A \in \mathbf{S}', B \in \mathbf{S}''\}$ of two segmentation. $\mathbf{S}' \wedge \mathbf{S}''$ is composed of all intersections of $\mathbf{S}'$ and $\mathbf{S}''$. The common refinement is as well, known as the *union segmentation* , because its segment boundary set is exactly the union of the boundaries of $\mathbf{S}'$ and $\mathbf{S}''$. Specifically, therefore $\mathbf{S} \wedge \mathbf{S} = \mathbf{S}$.

Now defining the *potential* of a segmentation $\mathbf{S}$ as

$$E(\mathbf{S}) = \sum_{A \in \mathbf{S}} \mathfrak{e}(A) \,, \tag{3}$$

where $\mathfrak{e}$ is a potential function which evaluate the one dimensional segmentation.

This gives rise to a class of distances between all segmentations defined by

$$D(\mathbf{S}', \mathbf{S}'') = E(\mathbf{S}') + E(\mathbf{S}'') - 2E(\mathbf{S}' \wedge \mathbf{S}'') \tag{4}$$

Substituting for D in equ.(2) yields

$$f(\mathbf{C}) = \sum_{q=1}^{m} w_q E(\mathbf{C}) + \sum_{q=1}^{m} w_q E(\mathbf{S_q}) - 2 \sum_{q=1}^{m} w_q E(\mathbf{C} \wedge \mathbf{S_q}) \tag{5}$$

where the middle term depends only on the input segmentation. It is therefore a constant that can be dropped for the purpose of optimization. Using the fact that the weights are normalized, we obtain the objective function

$$\tilde{f}(\mathbf{C}) := f(\mathbf{C}) - \sum_{q=1}^{m} w_q E(\mathbf{S_q}) = E(\mathbf{C}) - 2 \sum_{q=1}^{m} w_q E(\mathbf{C} \wedge \mathbf{S_q}) \tag{6}$$

Now we clearly consider $\mathbf{C}$ as a sequence of intervals A. Using the additivity of the potential E we obtain

$$\tilde{f}(\mathbf{C}) = \sum_{A \in \mathbf{C}} \left(\mathfrak{e}(A) - 2 \sum_{q=1}^{m} w_q \sum_{\substack{B \in \mathbf{S}_q \\ B \cap A \neq \varnothing}} \mathfrak{e}(A \cap B) \right) =: \sum_{A \in \mathbf{C}} \Delta(A) \tag{7}$$

The additive form of equ.(7) as a sum of the contributions $\Delta(A)$ for the consensus segments $\mathbf{C}$ makes it possible to minimize $\tilde{f}(\mathbf{C})$ using dynamic programming [Mielikäinen et al., 2006]. Consequently, consider the subset $\mathcal{C}_{|k}$ of segmentations that have a segment boundary at k, i.e., position k is the end point of a segment. For a given 1-D segmentation $\mathbf{C} \in \mathcal{C}_{|k}$, denote by $\tilde{f}(\mathbf{C}|k)$ the sum of the contributions $\Delta(A)$ with max $A \leq k$. Write $F_k := \min_{\mathbf{C} \in \mathcal{C}_{|k}} \tilde{f}(\mathbf{C}|k)$ for the minimal value of $\tilde{f}(\mathbf{C}|k)$. Since k is a segment boundary, the last segment A before k is necessarily of the form $[j+1, k]$, where $j < k$ denotes the segment boundary immediately preceding k. Using this equation, we can calculate

$$F_k = \min_{\mathbf{C} \in \mathcal{C}_{|k}} \tilde{f}(\mathbf{C}|k) = \min_{j<k} \min_{\mathbf{C} \in \mathcal{C}_{|j}} \left(\Delta([j+1,k]) + \tilde{f}(\mathbf{C}|j) \right)$$

$$= \min_{j<k} \left(\Delta([j+1,k]) + \min_{\mathbf{C} \in \mathcal{C}_{|j}} \tilde{f}(\mathbf{C}|j) \right) = \min_{j<k} \left(\Delta([j+1,k]) + F_j \right) \tag{8}$$

Therefore, we obtain a simple dynamic programming recursion that has the same form for weighted and un-weighted consensus segmentation, see also [Mielikäinen et al., 2006]. The weight only appears in the scoring function Δ. In addition, we noticed that recursion (8) is the same as the segmentation problem in [Bellman, 1961] in general. For example, for financial time series, it appears in [Bai and Perron, 2002], appears in [Fragkou et al., 2004] in the context of text segmentation, and is used to analyze arrays in [Picard et al., 2005] for CGH data, and in [Huber et al., 2006, Danford et al., 2011, Bischler et al., 2014] to identify transcripts in tiling arrays and RNA-seq data. This is discussed in the setting of the very general similarity measure in [Machné et al., 2017]. As we will see below, the work of calculating F_k is mainly the work of calculating the score $\Delta[i, j]$.

Before we proceed, we briefly define a general condition on the form of the potential function $\epsilon(\,.\,)$. Denote by $\mathbf{D}$ the discrete segmentation in which every input interval is a single point and by $\mathbf{J}$ the in-discrete segmentation $\mathbf{J}$ consisting of a single interval. A function ϵ is sub-additive if $\epsilon(A) \leq \epsilon(A_1) + \epsilon(A_2)$ for every A and every subdivision $A_1 \dot\cup A_2 = A$ of A. This inequality is strict for at least one interval if and only if $\epsilon([1, n]) < \sum_{i=1}^{n} \epsilon([i, i])$. Comparing $\mathbf{D}$ and $\mathbf{J}$, we observe that in this case $D(\mathbf{D}, \mathbf{J}) = \epsilon([1, n]) - \sum_{i=1}^{n}[i, i] < 0$, violating that D is a proper distance function. For the limiting case of an additive potential, $\epsilon(A) = \epsilon(A_1) + \epsilon(A_2)$ for all intervals and their subdivisions, we obtain $D(\mathbf{S}, \mathbf{S}') = 0$ for any two segmentations $\mathbf{S}$ and $\mathbf{S}'$. Thus only potentials that satisfy $\epsilon(A) > \epsilon(A_1) + \epsilon(A_2)$ for at least some $A_1 \dot\cup A_2 = A$ are of interest. A function is *super-additive* if $\epsilon(A) \geq \epsilon(A_1) + \epsilon(A_2)$ for all $A_1 \dot\cup A_2 = A$. One easily checks that D is a metric whenever ϵ is super-additive. This condition is not necessary, however. For example, the neg-entropy defined in equ.(17) below, is not super-additive.

5.2.2 Efficient computation of the segment scores $\Delta[i, j]$

The direct evaluation of $\Delta([i, k]$ according to its definition, equ.(8), for given i and k, requires $O(n\,m)$ operation because this entails the summation over $O(n)$ segments for each of the m input segmentations. This results in an impractical total effort of $O(n^3\,m)$ compared to the quadratic cost of the dynamic programming recursion itself. It is of considerable practical interest, accordingly, to find a more efficient way of calculation the scoring function. The key idea is to define, for a given position i, two

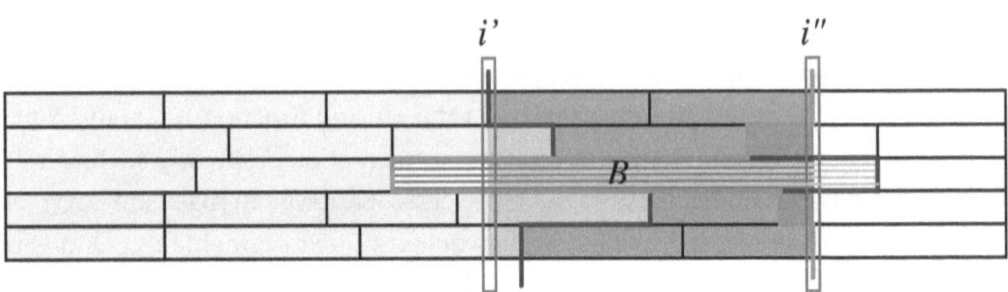

Figure 5.3: *Definition of auxiliary variables. The input segments contributing to $\delta_<(i'')$ are all those to the left of the green line (i.e., the ones shown in light and dark gray. $\delta_\leq(i')$ are to the left of the blue line, i.e, those shown in light gray. The large interval B is included in $\delta_\leq(i')$ but not in $\delta_<(i'')$. The correction terms $\delta_>^\cap(i')$ and $\delta_<^\cap(i'')$ comprise the cyan and magenta parts, respectively. The correction term $\delta^*(i',i'')$, finally adds takes care of the interval B.*

slightly different partial sums:

$$\delta_<(i) := \sum_{q=1}^{m} w_q \sum_{\substack{B \in S_q \\ \max B \leq i}} \mathfrak{e}(B) \quad \text{and} \quad \delta_\leq(i) := \sum_{q=1}^{m} w_q \sum_{\substack{B \in S_q \\ \min B \leq i}} \mathfrak{e}(B) \tag{9}$$

For a given boundary i in $\mathbf{C}$, the first term sums all intervals in $\mathbf{S}_q$ that do not extend beyond i, while the second sum also includes those that begin before or at i and extend beyond i. Thus $\delta_<(k) - \delta_\leq(j)$ captures all segments of the $\mathbf{S}_q$ that are contained within $[j+1,k]$ with one important exception: Segments such as B in Fig. 5.3 that contain $[j+1,k]$ contribute to $\delta_\leq(j)$ but not to $\delta_<(k)$. Such overlapping segments will be taken care of in a correction term discussed below. Using the notation $B_{\leq i} := \{b \in B | b \leq i\}$ and $B_{\geq i} := \{b \in B | b \geq i\}$ we furthermore define terms

$$\delta_<^\cap(i) := \sum_{q=1}^{m} w_q \sum_{\substack{B \in S_q \\ i \in B, i \neq \max B}} \mathfrak{e}(B_{\leq i}) \quad \text{and} \quad \delta_>^\cap(i) := \sum_{q=1}^{m} w_q \sum_{\substack{B \in S_q \\ i \in B, i \neq \min B}} \mathfrak{e}(B_{\geq i}) \tag{10}$$

where each sum contains at most a single term, namely the interval $B \in \mathbf{S}_q$ that extends across i. Note that intervals that begin or end in position i do not contribute to $\delta_>^\cap(i)$ or $\delta_<^\cap(i)$, respectively. The correction terms correspond to the parts of segments that are non-trivially intersected by $[j+1,k]$, shown in magenta and cyan, resp., in Fig. 5.3. Thus $\delta_<(k) - \delta_\leq(j) + \delta_<^\cap(k) + \delta_>^\cap(j+1)$ covers exactly all the intervals contributing to $[j+1,k]$ – with the exception of segments $B \in \mathcal{S}_q$ that begin at $\min B < j+1$ and end at $\max B > k$ as mentioned above. For such segments, instead of the contributions for $B_{\leq k}$ and $B_{\geq j+1}$ a single contribution for the interval $[j+1,k] \cap B = [j+1,k]$ has to be used. In addition, the contribution for B that is erroneously subtracted with $\delta_{\leq}(j)$, needs to be restored. Collecting these contributions, we obtain the following correction term for intervals that span across the interval $[i',i'']$ of interest:

$$\delta^*(i',i'') := \sum_{q=1}^{m} w_q \sum_{\substack{B \in \mathcal{S}_q \\ i',i'' \in B \\ \min B < i' \leq i'' < \max B}} \left(\mathbf{e}(B) + \mathbf{e}([i',i'']) - \mathbf{e}(B_{\leq i''}) - \mathbf{e}(B_{\geq i'}) \right) \tag{11}$$

For the interval $[j+1,k]$, the correction term $\delta^*(j+1,k-1)$ defined in equ.(11) can be understood as follows: the first term accounts for the correct contribution of $B \cap [j+1,k] = [j+1,k]$, the second term compensates for the error introduced by $\delta_{\leq}(j)$, and the remaining two terms remove the superfluous contributions introduced by $\delta_{\leq}^{\cap}(k)$ and $\delta_{>}^{\cap}(j+1)$. We summarize this derivation in the following form:

Theorem 1. *The potential-dependent segment scores defined in equ.(7) can be expressed as*

$$\Delta([j+1,k]) = \mathbf{e}([j+1,k]) - 2\left(\delta_{<}(k) - \delta_{\leq}(j) + \delta_{<}^{\cap}(k) + \delta_{>}^{\cap}(j+1) + \delta^*(j+1,k)\right) \tag{12}$$

The only term that depends on both $j+1$ and k is the correction of long input intervals $\delta^*(j+1,k)$. The restricted sum over the $B \in \mathbf{S}_q$ in equ.(11) contains at most one segment for each input segmentation and thus can be evaluated in $O(m)$ time for a given interval. Furthermore, the sum is certainly empty whenever $[j+1,k]$ is larger than the largest segment in any of the $\mathbf{S}_q$; this can be used to speed up the evaluation from $O(m)$ to $O(1)$ if the segment lengths in the input are bounded by a constant, except for the short intervals.

Lemma 1. *The arrays of correction terms $\delta_<$, $\delta_\leq$, $\delta_{<}^{\cap}$, and $\delta_{>}^{\cap}$ can be computed in $O(nm)$ total time.*

Proof. The values of $\delta_<(i)$ and $\delta_\leq(i)$ can be computed interactively: we obtain $\delta_<(i)$ by adding the contribution $w_q \mathbf{e}(B_q)$ to $\delta_<(i-1)$ whenever $i = \max B_q$ for the segmentation $\mathbf{S_q}$. Similarly, $\delta_\leq(i)$ is obtained by $w_q \mathbf{e}(B_q)$ to $\delta_\leq(i-1)$ if $i = \min B_q$. For each i, therefore, we require $O(m)$ operations. The sums in equ.(10) comprise at most one segment of S_q for every q. All terms can be computed in constant time using auxiliary arrays that return, for each i and q, the values of $\min B$ and $\max B$ for $i \in B$ and $B \in S_q$. These auxiliary arrays in turn can obviously be constructed in $O(nm)$ time for the breakpoints list of the input segmentations.

It therefore makes sense to precompute the arrays $\delta_<$, $\delta_\leq$, $\delta_<^\cap$, and $\delta_<^\cap(k)$.

Corollary 1. *The score $\Delta[j+1,k]$ can be computed in $O(m)$ time with $O(nm)$ preprocessing cost to compute the arrays $\delta_<$, $\delta_\leq$, $\delta_<^\cap$, and $\delta_>^\cap$.*

It is worth noting, finally, that there is nothing to be gained by storing the score values $\Delta[j+1,k]$ since each entry is used only once in the recursion.

5.2.3 Boundaries of Consensus Segments

For a function g on $\mathbb{Z}$ we define the local curvature at x as $\partial_x^2 g(x) := g(x+1) + g(x-1) - 2g(x)$. A function g is (strictly) *convex* at x if $\partial_x^2 g(x) > 0$. This condition immediately implies that x is not a local maximum of g since at least one of $g(x+1)$ or $g(x-1)$ is larger than $g(x)$. Correspondingly, g is (strictly) *concave* in x if $\partial_x^2 g(x) < 0$, whence x is not a local minimum.

Definition 1. *The potential $\mathfrak{e}$ is boundedly convex if satisfied for all intervals $p' \leq p \leq x \leq q \leq q'$*

$$\partial_x^2 \mathfrak{e}([x,q]) \geq \partial_x^2 \mathfrak{e}([x,q']) > 0 \quad and \quad \partial_x^2 \mathfrak{e}([p,x]) \geq \partial_x^2 \mathfrak{e}([p',x]) > 0. \tag{13}$$

For boundedly convex $\mathfrak{e}$, the curvature in non-increasing as the intervals become larger. In particular, suppose $\mathfrak{e}([p,q])$ depends only on the length $z := q - p + 1$ of the interval and is a smooth function, then $\mathfrak{e}''(z) > 0$ and $\mathfrak{e}'''(z) \leq 0$ for all $z > 0$ implies $\mathfrak{e}$ is boundedly convex.

Theorem 2. *Let $\{S_1, S_1, \ldots, S_m\}$ be a set of segmentations with union segmentation $\hat{S}$ and suppose $\mathfrak{e}$ is boundedly convex. Then the consensus C is refined by the union segmentation $\hat{S}$.*

Proof. Following [Mielikäinen et al., 2006, Terzi, 2006] we assume, for contradiction, that the optimal consensus C has a segment boundary $\hat{j}$ that is not contained in the union segmentation $\hat{S}$. We aim to show that moving $\hat{j}$ to some close-by position x

will reduce the cost $f(\mathbf{C})$. Fix an input segmentation $\mathbf{S}_q$ and denote by $\hat{\mathbf{S}}_\mathbf{q} := \mathbf{S}_\mathbf{q} \wedge \mathbf{C}$. Denote by $p - 1$ and q the first boundaries to the left and to the right of $\hat{\jmath}$ in $\mathbf{C}$. Analogously, $\hat{p}$ and $\hat{q}$ are the first boundary to the left and to the right of $\hat{\jmath}$ in $\hat{\mathbf{S}}_\mathbf{q}$, respectively. Thus $\mathbf{C}$ contains the two segments $[p, \hat{\jmath}]$ and $[\hat{\jmath} + 1, q]$. Since every segment of $\hat{\mathbf{S}}_\mathbf{q} \wedge \mathbf{C}$ is a subset of a unique segment of $\mathbf{C}$, we have $[\hat{p}, \hat{q}] \subseteq [p, q]$.

We proceed by evaluating how $D(\mathbf{S}_\mathbf{q}, \mathbf{C}) = E(\mathbf{S}_\mathbf{q}) + E(\mathbf{C}) - 2E(\mathbf{S}_\mathbf{q} \wedge \mathbf{C})$ varies when the boundary $\hat{\jmath}$ is perturbed. Let x be the perturbed boundary position. Since only $E(\mathbf{C})$ and $2E(\mathbf{S}_\mathbf{q} \wedge \mathbf{C})$ depends on x and all boundaries except $\hat{\jmath}$ are fixed, it suffices to focus on the intervals $[p, q]$ and $[\hat{p}, \hat{q}]$, respectively. Collecting all constant terms in D_0 we obtain

$$D(x) = D_0 + \mathfrak{e}([p, x]) + \mathfrak{e}([x + 1, q]) - 2\mathfrak{e}([\hat{p}, x]) - 2\mathfrak{e}([x + 1, \hat{q}]) \qquad (14)$$

Since $\mathfrak{e}$ is boundedly convex, we have $0 < \partial_x^2 \mathfrak{e}([p, x]) \leq \partial_x^2 \mathfrak{e}([\hat{p}, x])$ and $0 < \partial_x^2 \mathfrak{e}([x + 1, q]) \leq \partial_x^2 \mathfrak{e}([x + 1, \hat{q}])$, whence $\partial_x^2 D(x) < -\partial_x^2 \mathfrak{e}([\hat{p}, x]) - \partial_x^2 \mathfrak{e}([x + 1, \hat{q}]) < 0$. Thus $D(x)$ is concave at x for every $\mathbf{S}_\mathbf{q}$ and thus also for any non-negative contribution to the linear combination of input segmentations. Thus, $f(\mathbf{C})$ as a function of the moving boundary x cannot have a minimum in the interior of the interval $[\hat{p}, \hat{q}]$, contradicting the assumption that $\hat{\jmath}$ is a boundary in the optimal consensus $\mathbf{C}$.

Thm. 2 establishes a very useful property: All segment boundaries of the consensus are contained in the union segmentation. This property was observed for disagreement distance and information distance (see below) in the unweighted setting [Mielikäinen et al., 2006, Terzi, 2006]. Here we show it holds for a broader class of distance functions and arbitrary weighting schemes. The techniques used in the proof of Thm. 2 do not seem to generalize to potentials with increasing curvature. Numerical data, however, indicate that the union segmentation refines the consensus for a much larger class of potential functions.

From an algorithmic point of view it implies that it suffices to compute the F_k for those values of k where segment boundaries are in the union segmentation of the inputs $\hat{\mathbf{S}}$. Correspondingly, we need to store the auxiliary variables only for the intervals of the union segmentation, instead of each i. That is, the recursion (8) reduced to

$$F_{j_k} = \min_{\substack{i < k \\ j_i \in \partial \hat{\mathbf{S}}}} \left(\Delta([j_i + 1, j_k]) + F_{j_i} \right) \qquad (15)$$

where $j_i \in \partial \hat{\mathbf{S}}$ denotes the i-th segment boundary in the union segmentation $\hat{\mathbf{S}}$.

Recursion (15) also speeds up the computation of the scoring function Δ, which now is also needed only for the segment boundaries. First note that we still obtain $\delta_<(i_k)$ from $\delta_<(i_{k-1})$ by adding the contributions $e(B)$ for the intervals ending at the boundary i_k to $\delta_<(i_{k-1})$ since by definition i_{k-1} and i_k are consecutive breakpoints. Analogously, $\delta_>(i_k)$ is obtained by adding $e(B)$ for all blocks beginning at i_{k-1} to $\delta_>(i_{k-1})$. The terms $\delta_>^\cap(i_k)$ and $\delta_<^\cap(i_k)$ remain the same. The correction term δ^* could be stored for all pairs of the boundaries in $\hat{\mathbf{S}}$. Alternatively, it suffices to store the m boundaries at which the intervals crossing i_k start and to keep track of the correct correction term directly in recursion (15). Equ.(15) thus can be evaluated in $O(s^2)$, where s is the number of breakpoints in the union segmentation.

5.2.4 Length Bounds on Consensus Segments

It is reasonable to expect that a consensus segmentation cannot be a lot coarser than the individual input segmentations. To see that this is indeed the case we start with a technical observation.

Lemma 2. *Consider intervals* $A = [i,k]$, $A' = [i,x]$ *and* $A'' = [x+1,k]$. *Then* $\Delta(A) > \Delta(A') + \Delta(A'')$ *if for every* $\mathbf{S_q}$ *there is* $B \in \mathbf{S_q}$ *with* $x \in B$ *such that*

$$e(A) - \left(e(A') + e(A'')\right) > 2\left[e(B) - \left(e(B \cap A') + e(B \cap A'')\right)\right] \tag{16}$$

Proof. Equ.(7) implicitly defined $\Delta(A)$ as the term in parentheses, which in turn is the w_q-weighted sum of contributions for each $\mathbf{S_q}$. Consider $B \in \mathbf{S_q}$ with $B \subset A$. The contribution $d_q(A)$ of $\mathbf{S_q}$ to $\Delta(A)$ is

$$
\begin{aligned}
d_q(A) \;&=\; e(A) - 2 \sum_{B' \in \mathbf{S_q}} e(A \cap B') \\[2mm]
&=\; e(A) - 2\left(\sum_{\substack{B' \in \mathbf{S_q}: \\ \max B' < \max B}} e(A \cap B') + \sum_{\substack{B' \in \mathbf{S_q} \\ \max B' > \max B}} e(A \cap B') \right) - 2e(B)
\end{aligned}
$$

Now consider an alternative segmentation in which A is subdivided into $A' \dot\cup A''$ at some position x inside B. Then A contributes

$$d_q(A') + d_q(A'') \; = \; \mathfrak{e}(A') + \mathfrak{e}(A'') - 2\left(\mathfrak{e}(A' \cap B) + \mathfrak{e}(A'' \cap B)\right)$$

$$-2\left(\sum_{\substack{B' \in \mathbf{S_q}: \\ \max B' < \max B}} \mathfrak{e}(A' \cap B') + \sum_{\substack{B' \in \mathbf{S_q} \\ \max B' > \max B}} \mathfrak{e}(A'' \cap B')\right)$$

The terms corresponding the segments $B' \neq B$ that intersect A are the same as before since either $B' \cap A = B' \cap A'$ or $B' \cap A = B' \cap A''$, depending on whether B' comes before or after B in $\mathbf{S_q}$. Thus we have $d_q(A) > d_q(A') + d_q(A')$ if and only if equ.(16) is satisfied. Since $\Delta(A)$, $\Delta(A')$, and $\Delta(A'')$ are convex linear combinations of the $d_q(A)$, $d_q(A')$, and $d_q(A'')$, respectively, it is sufficient for $\Delta(A) > \Delta(A') + \Delta(A'')$ that $d_q(A) > d_q(A') + d_q(A')$ holds for all $\mathbf{S_q}$. In other words, if A satisfies the condition of Lemma 2, then $\tilde{f}(\mathbf{C})$ strictly decreases when A is subdivided into A' and A''. Thus we conclude

Corollary 2. *An interval A satisfying the conditions specified in Lemma 2 cannot appear in a consensus segmentation.*

Our goal is now to show that sufficiently long intervals A always satisfy the conditions of Lemma 2 and thus can never be part of the consensus segmentation. Here we need that $\mathfrak{e}$ is superadditive, i.e., $\mathfrak{e}(A) > e(A_1) + e(A_2)$ for all $A = A_1 \dot\cup A_2$ and $A_1, A_2 \neq \varnothing$. This is the case in particular for the polynomial potentials. It fails for the negentropy potential, equ.(17), however, because this function is not monotonically increasing with the segment length $|A|$.

Theorem 3. *Let $\mathfrak{e}$ be a superadditive potential. Let B be the longest segment in the input segmentations and denote by ℓ^* the length of the shortest interval A such that $\mathfrak{e}(A) - 2\mathfrak{e}(A') > 2\mathfrak{e}(B) - 2\min_{B',B'':B'\cup B''=B}(\mathfrak{e}(B') + \mathfrak{e}(B''))$, where $|A'| = \lceil |A|/2 \rceil$ and $|B'| = \lfloor |B|/2 \rfloor$. Then every segment of the consensus segmentation is shorter than $L^* := \max(2|B|, \ell^*)$.*

Proof. If $\mathfrak{e}$ is superadditive, the l.h.s. of equ.(16) is maximal if $|A'| = |A''|$ (for even $|A|$) or $|A'| = |A''| \pm 1$ for odd $|A|$, i.e., we assume that x is located in the middle of A. In order to ensure that segments containing x are completely contained in A we need $|A| \geq 2|B|$. If this condition is satisfied, equ.(16) applies. We obtain a sufficient condition by replacing the r.h.s. with the maximal possible contribution of the subdivided interval B. By superadditivity, this term monotonically increases with the size of B. The assumption that x equally divides A fixed the l.h.s. of the inequality. Since $\mathfrak{e}$ is strictly superadditive $\mathfrak{e}(A) - 2\mathfrak{e}(A')$ is strictly monotonically increasing with $|A|$ and thus there is a unique smallest value ℓ^* of $|A|$ unless $\mathfrak{e}(A) - 2\mathfrak{e}(A') \leq 2$ for all A, in which case no bound ℓ^* exists.

Corollary 3. *The consensus segmentation* **C** *with superadditive potential $\mathfrak{e}$ for m input segmentations with length bound L^* as specified in Thm. 3 can be computed in $O(nmL^*)$ time.*

Proof. We observe that for each k, only values of j between $k - 2\ell^*$ and $k - 1$ appear in equ.(8) since longer segments by Thm. 3 cannot be part of an optimal consensus segmentation. The corollary now follows immediately from Cor. 1.

The length bound on consensus segments thus leads to a reduction of the computational efforts. Although ℓ^* in Thm. 3 may be inconvenient to compute for some choices of the potential $\mathfrak{e}$, we shall see below that a simple, uniform bound can be obtained for an interesting class of potentials.

5.2.5 Special Potential Functions

Let us now consider plausible distance functions. The *disagreement distance* between segmentation was introduced in [Mielikäinen et al., 2006] using the potential $\mathfrak{e}(A) := (|A|/n)^2/2$. A natural generalization is $\mathfrak{e}(A) = (|A|/n)^{1+\alpha}/(1 + \alpha)$ for $0 < \alpha \leq 1$. We note that a linear potential $\mathfrak{e}(|A|) = |A|/n$, i.e., $\alpha = 0$, yields a constant value of $\tilde{f}(\mathbf{C})$ because the sum of all segment lengths adds up to n and thus $E(\mathbf{S}) = 1$ is independent of the segmentation $\mathbf{S}$.

Recall that the entropy of a discrete distribution is defined as $H = -\sum_i p_i \ln p_i$. Given a segmentation $\mathbf{S}$, we consider the probabilities p_i of randomly picking a point from a segment, i.e., $p_i = |A_i|/n$ is the relative length of a segment $A_i \in \mathbf{S}$, where n denotes the total length of the segmented genome or time series. The *information distance* is the symmetrized conditional entropy, which can also be computed as $D(\mathbf{S}', \mathbf{S}'') = 2H(\mathbf{S}' \wedge \mathbf{S}'') - H(\mathbf{S}') - H(\mathbf{S}'')$ [Mielikäinen et al., 2006, Haiminen et al., 2007]. It corresponds to the potential function

$$\mathfrak{e}(A) := (|A|/n) \ln(|A|/n) \tag{17}$$

given by the negative of the entropy (negentropy) contribution of the interval A.
It has been shown in [Mielikäinen et al., 2006, Terzi, 2006] that $\hat{S}$ refines the un-weighted consensus segmentation for both the disagreement distance and the information distance. This result generalizes to the weighted case and the α-disagreement distances with $0 < \alpha \leq 1$.

Corollary 4. *The consensus segmentation* $\mathbf{C}$ *is refined by the union segmentation* $\hat{S}$ *for the disagreement distance, its α generalization with $0 < \alpha \leq 1$, as well as the information distance.*

Proof. It suffices to show that the potentials $\epsilon(z)$ are boundedly convex. For the disagreement distance we have $\epsilon(z) = z^2/2$ we have $\epsilon''(z) = 1$ and $\epsilon'''(z) = 0$; for $\epsilon(z) = z^{1+\alpha}/(1-\alpha)$ we have $\epsilon''(z) = \alpha z^{\alpha-1} > 0$ and $\epsilon'''(z) = \alpha(\alpha-1)z^{\alpha-2} < 0$ for $0 < \alpha \leq 1$. For the negentropy, $\epsilon(z) = z \ln z$, we have $\epsilon''(z) = 1/z > 0$ and $\epsilon'''(z) = -1/z^2 < 0$ where $z := (|A|/n)$. The scaling by $1/n$ obviously does not affect the signs. Is does not seem possible to generalize the result to potentials that grow faster than quadratically. Let us finally consider the consequence of Thm. 3. Reusing the convexity results above we can replace $2 \min_{B',B'':B'\cup B''=B}(\epsilon(B') + \epsilon(B''))$ by $4\epsilon(B')$ where $|B'| = \lfloor|B|/2\rfloor$. A short computation then shows that the inequality in Thm. 3 is satisfied for $|A| > {}^{1+\alpha}\!\sqrt{2}|B|$. Since ${}^{1+\alpha}\!\sqrt{2} \leq 2$ we have

Corollary 5. *The consensus segmentation* $\mathbf{C}$ *of a collection of segmentations* $\mathbf{S_q}$ *with respect to the α-disagreement potentials contains no segment longer than twice the length of the longest input segment.*

This allows us immediately to limit the range of the indices in recursion (8) to $j_i > j_k - 2 \max |B|$.

5.2.6 Generalization: Symmetrized Boundary Mover's Distance

Equ.(7) highlights the fact that the cost function $\tilde{f}(\mathbf{C})$ measures, for each segment $A \in \mathbf{C}$, how well A conforms to the input segmentations. As noted above, the additive structure of equ.(7) is sufficient to enable minimization by dynamic programming for arbitrary choices of Δ. If we retain the idea of weighted contributions for each input segmentation, we may write $\Delta(A) = \sum_q w_q \Delta(A|\mathbf{S}_q)$, where $\Delta(A|\mathbf{S}_q)$ measures how well the segment A "fits" into the segmentation $\mathbf{S}_q$. As a minimal requirement, for any given interval A, the score $\Delta(A|\mathbf{S}_q)$ must attain its minimum value if the interval

A is a segment in $\mathbf{S}_q$. Since two segmentations in general do not have segments or breakpoints in common, measures are required that are more fine-grained than the distinction between identical and distinct segments or breakpoints. $\Delta(A|\mathbf{S}_q)$ thus are similar to a measure of overlap, between A and the segments of $\mathbf{S}_q$ that are covered by A. Clearly the potential-based measures can be understood in this manner.

An interesting class of dissimilarities utilizes the distance between break points instead of the lengths of intersections between segments. For a segmentation $\mathbf{S}$ with segments S_i, $i = 1,\ldots,n$, we define $s_i = \max S_i$ and set $s_0 = 0$, i.e., the segments are $S_i = [s_{i-1} + 1, s_i] =: (s_{i-1}..s_i)$. By slight abuse of notation we write $\mathbf{S} = (s_0, s_1, \ldots, s_m)$, i.e., we now specify a segmentation in terms of its breakpoints. Moreover, we write $s \in \mathbf{S}$ to mean that s represents a breakpoint in the segmentation $\mathbf{S}$.

The *"boundary movers distance"* was introduced in [Mielikäinen et al., 2006, Terzi, 2006] as

$$D_B(\mathbf{S}|\mathbf{C}) := \sum_{s \in \mathbf{S}} \min_{c \in \mathbf{C}} d(s, c), \tag{18}$$

where $d(.,.)$ is some distance function between the positions s and c on $[1,\ldots,n]$. The dissimilarity measure D_B is not symmetric and satisfies $D_B(\mathbf{S}|\mathbf{C}) = 0$ whenever $\mathbf{C}$ is a refinement of $\mathbf{S}$. The segmentation aggregation problem minimizing $\sum_q w_q D_B(\mathbf{S_q}|\mathbf{C})$ is therefore solved by the union segmentation $\mathbf{C} = \hat{\mathbf{S}}$, while $\sum_q w_q D_B(\mathbf{C}|\mathbf{S_q})$ is minimized by the indiscrete segmentation $\{[1,n]\}$. As noted in [Mielikäinen et al., 2006, Terzi, 2006], these measures thus are only useful with additional constraints on the number or size of allowed segments.

The symmetrized version of D_B, however, has attractive properties for our purposes, as we shall see: Clearly, $\min_{c \in \mathbf{C}} d(s, c) = \min\{d(s, c'), d(s, c'')\}$, where c' and c'' delimit the segment of $\mathbf{C}$ within which s resides. If $s = c'$ or $s = c''$, the contribution vanishes, hence we can write

$$D_B(\mathbf{S}|\mathbf{C}) := \sum_{(c'..c'') \in \mathbf{C}} \sum_{s \in (c'..c'')} \min\{d(s, c'), d(s, c'')\} \tag{19}$$

This term individually penalizes a segment (c', c'') of $\mathbf{C}$ for containing boundary points of $\mathbf{S}$ in its interior. On the other hand, we can rewrite $D_B(\mathbf{C}|\mathbf{S})$ in terms of segments of $\mathbf{C}$ by simply splitting the contribution of each boundary between the two adjacent segments:

$$D_B(\mathbf{C}|\mathbf{S}) = \sum_{(c',c'')\in\mathbf{C}} \frac{1}{2}\left(\min_{s\in\mathbf{S}} d(s,c') + \min_{s\in\mathbf{S}} d(s,c'')\right) \tag{20}$$

Here, we have used that the lower boundary of the first segment and the upper boundary of the last segment must coincide (they are the boundaries of the interval where our segment is located), so they are not helpful for distance. Similarly, for each given value of c' or c'', the minimum value only takes over the two alternative breakpoints of $\mathbf{S}$, that is, those sections that define $\mathbf{S}$ the breakpoints of the boundary consensus segment are c' and c''. It is not difficult to see that $D(\mathbf{S},\mathbf{C}) = D_B(\mathbf{S}|\mathbf{C}) + D_B(\mathbf{C}|\mathbf{S})$ only disappear if $\mathbf{S} = \mathbf{C}$. In addition, $D_B(\mathbf{S}_q|\mathbf{C}) + D_B(\mathbf{C}|\mathbf{S}_q)$ can be written as a sum of contributions

$$\Delta_q((c'..c'')) := \sum_{\substack{s\in\mathbf{S}_q \\ s\in(c'..c'')}} \min\{d(s,c'), d(s,c'')\} + \frac{1}{2}\min_{s\in\mathbf{S}_q} d(s,c') + \frac{1}{2}\min_{s\in\mathbf{S}_q} d(s,c'') \tag{21}$$

For each segment $(c',c'') \in \mathbf{C}$ and each segment of input segmentation $\mathbf{S}_q$. Obviously, $\Delta((c'..c'')) = \sum_q w_q \Delta_q((c'..c''))$ depends only on the input segmentation $\mathbf{S}_q$ and the boundary Breakpoints c'' and c'', that is, a single segment in the consensus $\mathbf{C}$. Therefore, the segmentation aggregation problem with symmetrical boundaries mover distance can be solved again by dynamic programming recursion equ.(8). A deeper analysis of this distance function is the subject of ongoing research.

5.3 Computational Results

5.3.1 Implementation

The consensus segmentation algorithm can be obtained as R package *consseg*, in which dynamic programming recursion is implemented through *C++* via *Rcpp* ($\geq$ 0.12.18) and *RcppXPtrUtils* ($\geq$ 0.1.1) allows users to define potential functions. The CRAN software package provided with this contribution will also be available soon. The development version is available at https://github.com/Bierinformatik/consseg.

The input segmentations are converted into an index, which returns the minimum position $\min B_q$ and the maximum position $\max B_q$ for each position k of the segment B_q containing k. With their help, if $k = \max B_q$, then $w_q\mathfrak{e}(B_q)$ is added to $\delta_<(k-1)$ to get $\delta_<(k)$.

Similarly, whenever $k = \min B_q$, by adding $w_q\mathfrak{e}(B_q)$ to $\delta_\leq(k)$ to calculate $\delta_\leq(k)$.

The terms $\delta_\lesssim^\cap(k)$ and $\delta_\gtrsim^\cap(k)$ follow the equ.(10). These calculations are interleaved with the evaluation of the F_k equ.(8).

Since the most expensive part of the algorithm is the evaluation of the segment cost $\Delta[j+1,k]$, we store the value $J[k]$ of the segment boundary j to avoid their recalculation in the backtracking step. realizes the minimum value of the equ.(8) for position k.

Therefore, the last segment of the best segmentation on $[1,k]$ is $[J[k]+1,k]$. Then go back on $[1, J[k]]$. Therefore, $j_{i+1} = J[j_i]$ is used to obtain the optimal segmentation boundary, starting from $j_0 = n$ and continuing until reaching $j_k = 0$. It is worth noting that due to the calculation of the difference $\delta_<(k) - \delta_\leq(j)$ of two sums , for a large n and a very fast-growing potential $\mathfrak{e}$, the fast-increasing equ.(12) is easy to give up Into the error.

5.3.2 Consensus segmentation of yeast transcriptome data

In order to prove the usefulness of consensus segmentations, we explored the yeast transcriptome time series mentioned in the introduction. We calculated the subdivision consensus obtained using very different parameter selection [Machné et al., 2017]. We found that consensus segmentation seems to produce a strong representation of the transcriptome, and seems to be more suitable for the current annotation of the yeast genome than any particular choice of segmentation parameters. The example in Fig. 5.4 also shows that it is easy to detect different non-coding components, such as SRG1. Short segments with very low coverage may be gaps between transcriptome units without related RNA products. On the other hand, even low-expressed consistent detection elements may require careful inspection.

In order to evaluate the usefulness of consensus segmentation in a more quantitative way, we quantified the overlap of segments with annotated coding sequences. To this end, we determine the segment with the largest Jaccard index $B(C)$ for each CDS C, and then record the ratio of segment length to comment length $r(C)$. In symbols:

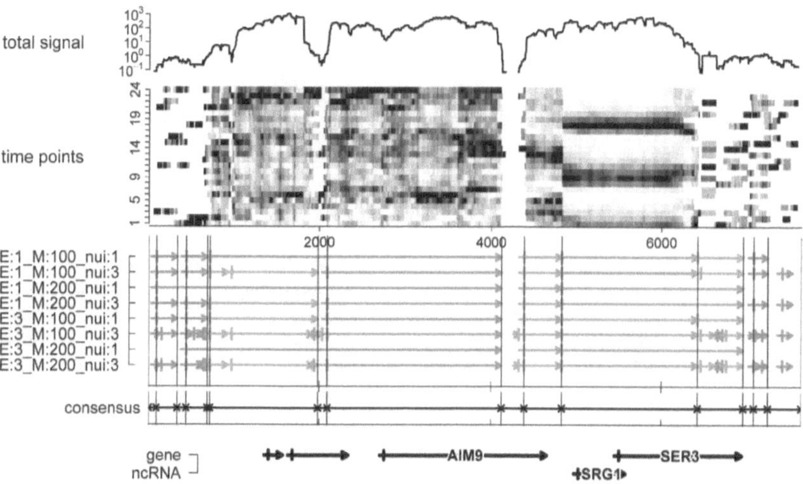

Figure 5.4: Alternative segmentations of yeast transcriptome data shown in Fig. 5.1 (here, the coverage time-series is shown as gray-values and the logarithms of the total coverage). Below, we show eight alternative segmentations computed with segmenTier [Machné et al., 2017] with different parameter settings. The consensus segments, computed for potential $\mathfrak{e}(z) = z^2/2$, match very well with the expectations from visual inspection of the data and from the annotation of yeast the genome (bottom). SRG1 is a non-coding RNA that represses the adjacent SER3 gene by transcriptional interference [Martens et al., 2004].

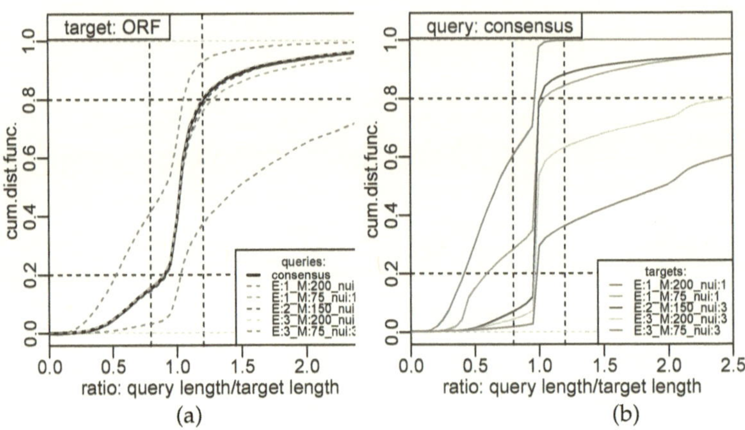

Figure 5.5: *Quantitative evaluation of the consensus of genome-wide transcriptome segmentations of RNA-seq data from S. cerevisae from ref. [Machné et al., 2017]. (a) Cumulative distribution function of the length ratios r between overlapping segments and previously annotated ORF transcripts [Xu et al., 2009]. A ratio of r = 1 indicates a good match. The consensus (black solid line) of five representative segmentations (colored dashed lines) by* segmenTier *with widely different parameter settings (as indicated in Fig. 2d of [Machné et al., 2017]) is at least on par with the best individual segmentation. (b) overlap of the consensus with the five different input segmentations. The individual segmentations share between about 30% and 70% of their segments with the consensus (vertical jump at r = 1). The consensus was computed with* $\mathfrak{e}(z) = z^2/2$.

$$r(C) := |B(C)|/|C| \quad \text{with} \quad B(C) := \arg\max_{B \in S} \frac{|B \cap C|}{|B \cup C|} \tag{22}$$

The cumulative distribution function $\text{cdf}(r)$ calculated on a large number of known transcripts C quantifies the consistency between segmentation and annotation. For reference, we use here a transcript containing the coding sequence annotated in [Xu et al., 2009]. $r = 1$ represents a perfect overlap between the consensus segment and the annotated transcript, $r < 1$ represents a shorter segment, and $r > 1$ represents a longer segment than the annotated transcript. Fig. 5.5(a) shows the $\text{cdf}(r)$ of 5151 CDS of *S. cerevisae* IFO 0233. These five segments have different parameters. These parameters are calculated with segmenTier [Machné et al., 2017]. The red curve is the consensus of these segmentations. It shows that consensus segmentation is

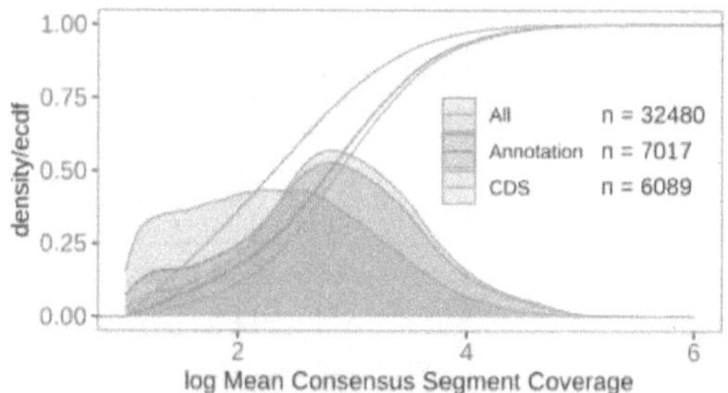

Figure 5.6: Distribution of RNA expression across the consensus segmentation of S. IFO 0233. We distinguish between coding sequences (CDS) with overlapping sequences or other annotation items (other) existing in the current genome annotation currently obtained from cerevisae and unannotated segments. There must be at least 30% overlap with the noted item. The density of each category is standardized to 1. Cumulative distribution is superimposed.

a reliable method: it is calculated from a small number of different segmentation samples, some of them are not particularly good, and its performance is at least as good as the best individual obtained by extensive search in the parameter space Segmentation is just as good [Machné et al., 2017]. The difference between annotation and consensus is not only the limitation of the segmentation method, but also stems from the inaccuracy of annotation, the processing of transcripts, and the complexity of the yeast transcriptome, which has a large amount of overlap and polycistronic transcripts [Pelechano et al., 2013]. The consensus performance is as good as the best individual segmentation (according to the benchmark in [Machné et al., 2017]). Fig. 5.5(b) shows that the share of each subdivision and consensus is between about 30% and 70% of the segmentation (corresponding to the vertical jump height of $r = 1$), that is, the consensus cannot simply summarize any single input breakdown. Therefore, we advocate the use of consensus segmentation as a robust and insensitive method to basic parameters for transcriptome analysis in compact genomes.

The consensus segmentation of the transcriptome of *S. cerevisae* IFO 0233 includes 74091 fragments. After filtering the spacer using the input segmentations [Machné et al., 2017] and very short fragments (most likely corresponding to small overlap and noise in the RNA-seq data), we retained 32,480 fragments. Figure 5.6 shows the distribution of median coverage. Not surprisingly, segments that overlap with known protein coding sequences (CDS) showed higher expression levels than other segments. Many segments overlap with various types of long non-coding RNAs, such as CUT and SUT [Parker et al., 2018, Till et al., 2018]. We have also observed many segments with substantial expression levels. So far, these segments have not been annotated, thus providing a large number of candidates for new ncRNAs. Transcriptome segmentation is only the first step towards accurate and reliable genome annotation. However, the subsequent processing of segmented data is beyond the scope of this contribution and will be resolved in future work.

5.3.3 Consensus segmentations of growth curves

The use of consensus fragments is by no means limited to transcriptome data or genomic fragments. Therefore, we also include a very different application here. The growth of the bacterial population over the time can be quantified by measuring the apparent absorption (often called OD (Optical Density)) in a spectrophotometer. Growth curves usually show different growth patterns: an initial time lag before the exponential growth phase, and then a deceleration phase that finally stabilizes to saturation,see e.g. [Hall et al., 2014]. They can be separated by approximating the time course of $\log OD$ with a series of line segments (ie, as a continuous piecewise linear function). The corresponding approximation problem is again a segmentation problem that can be solved by dynamic programming [Bellman, 1961]. Empirically, it has been observed that the resulting segmentation is very sensitive to the nuances of the growth curve. We show here that consensus segmentation is a convenient way to extract reliable estimates of the duration of different phases.

In the Fig. 5.7, we compare the growth curves of four *Escherichia coli* cultures grown in minimal glucose medium at 37 °C. R package dpseg [Machné and Stadler, 2020] is used to segment each growth curve. The algorithm also uses dynamic programming methods. Instead of fixing the number of segments as in [Bellman, 1961], it is better to use the penalty parameter to adjust the resolution of the segmentation. Compared with the segments of the average growth curve, the data can be viewed more intuitively, taking into account the consensus of each segment and the change of breakpoints between replications.

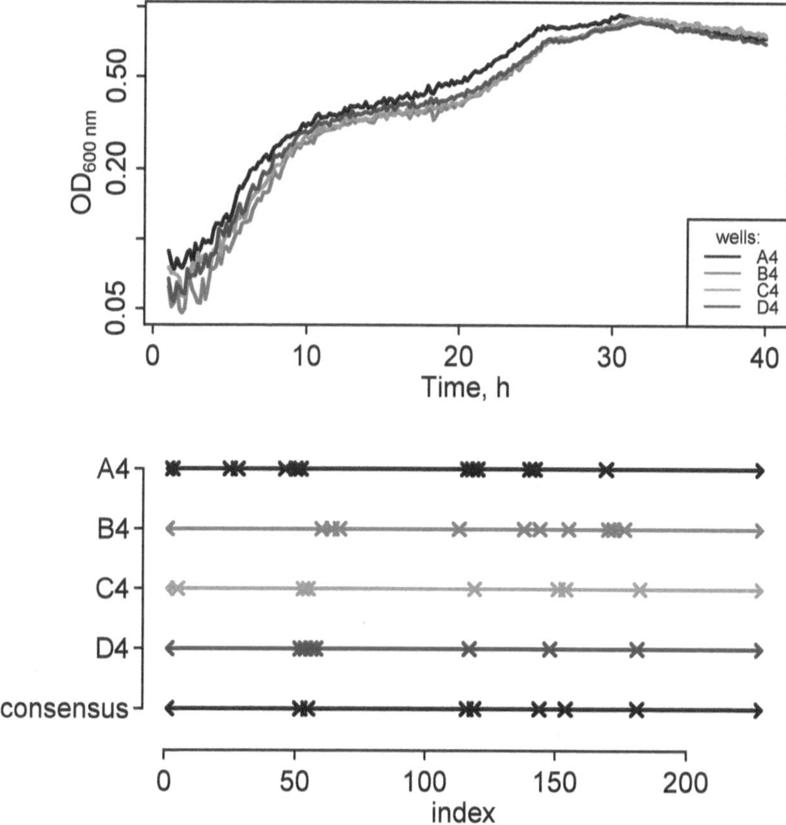

Figure 5.7: *Four Escherichia coli cultures were grown at identical conditions (four replicates in a larger experiment) in M9 medium with 0.2% glucose at 37°C in a BMG Clariostar platereader and the optical density at 600 nm, $\ln(OD_{600\,nm}$ was measured every 10 minutes. The growth curves of each of the four replicates were segmented into intervals with constant slope by the `dpseg` algorithm with the default jump penalty parameter $P = 0$ [Machné and Stadler, 2020].*

5.3.4   Refinement Conjecture

Thm. 2 pointed out that the union segmentation $\hat{S}$ completes the consensus segmentation of the bounded convex consensus function class C. Numerical simulations strongly show that although the proof technique has proven to fail in general, it is also true for many potentials with positive curvature increase. We use the base-R *sample* function to randomly select breakpoints within a given range, and simulate 10 segmentations of length 50 and a maximum of 10 segments. Fig. 5.8 shows the consensus segmentation for six potential functions from negentropy to exponential. We found that the consensus segment only contains breakpoints that exist in at least one input segment. This indicates:

Conjecture 1. $\hat{S}$ *appears to refine* C *for all superadditive potentials and possibly even for all convex potentials.*

This "Refinement Conjecture" has considerable practical uses. If true (assumed to be heuristic), it reduces the amount of calculation to $O(s^2)$ where s is the number of break points in the input segmentations. We have further observed a trend of faster growth potential, higher returns, and a shorter consensus interval. This is consistent with the fact that the bound $^{1+\alpha}\sqrt{2}|B|$ on the length of the consensus intervals in the argument leading up Cor. 5 decreases with the exponent α of the polynomial potentials.

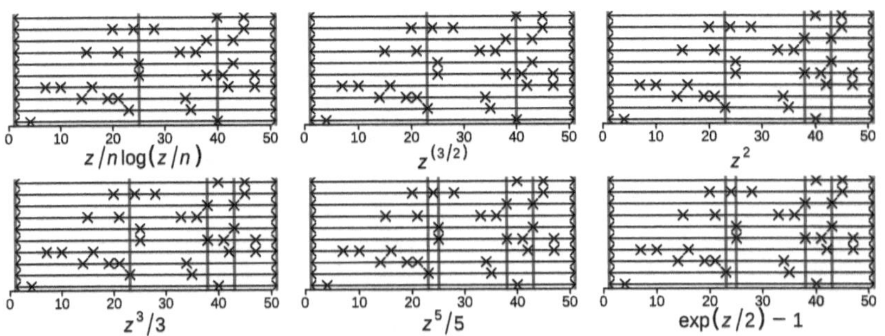

Figure 5.8: *For six different potential functions* $\mathfrak{e}(z)$, *the consensus segmentation of a set of 10 random segmentations with equal weights (shown by the blue vertical line). Please note that there are only breakpoints in the input segment (shown as × appear in the consensus segmentation)*

5.4 Concluding Remarks

In this work, we extend the previous work of [Mielikäinen et al., 2006, Terzi, 2006] on the problem of segmented aggregation and generalize it. We show that for a class of boundedly convex potential functions, including negative entropy and power functions $z^{1+\alpha}$ with $0 < \alpha \leq 1$, all consensus breakpoints are at least one contributing Breakpoints in the segmentations. In addition, we show that for all super-additive potentials, the length of the consensus segment cannot exceed twice the length of the longest input segment. This limit allows to further reduce the amount of calculation. The consensus segmentation described in this chapter involves two main application scenarios: (i) Coordination and Reconciliation of multi-dimensional data segmentation, including, for example, independent measurement (such as biological or technical duplication) or different amounts of measurement (such as different histone modifications). (ii) Reconcile the segmentation of the same dataset generated using different similarity measures.

In principle, the same similarity measure can also be used to calculate consensus segmentation for different segmentation generated using random algorithms or different heuristics. One of the main advantages of consensus segmentation is that it can be calculated without requiring specific information about the underlying data of the input segmentation. This knowledge is not needed, because the segmentation aggregation problem only depends on the distance function D as the "parameter". Based on experience, we have found that the change of the distance function has only a very moderate result on consensus segmentation.

In the simulation, we found strong support for the "Refinement Conjecture". This give support for the use of dynamic programming segmentation methods to select the best segmentation method from union segmentation calculated using different heuristic methods. Such a scheme has been proposed in [Pierre-Jean et al., 2015]. Compared with fully dynamic programming segmentation, this way can potentially gain substantial gains in computational efficiency. C-KS method [Toloşi et al., 2013] also restricts itself to union segmentation.

We considered two very different applications scenarios. Especially in the application of transcriptome data, consensus segmentation may significantly improve annotation. A special advantage of the consensus method is that by highlighting consistent differences between data tracks, processing related boundaries can be identified. This is particularly useful for organisms with operons, polycistronic primary transcripts, or genes with no expression or gaps between genes. In all these cases, it becomes difficult and often impossible to distinguish the transcription unit from the pattern of individually mapped RNA-seq reads. Here, we used data from the yeast strain IFO 0233, which was previously used to illustrate the transcriptome segmentation in [Machné et al., 2017]. We have seen that consensus segmentation can provide reliable predictions of transcriptome units from a moderate number of single segmentation with very different variables parameters. We got thousands of segments, which may correspond to non-coding transcripts in *S. cerevisae* IFO 0233. Since this algorithm aims to describe the method of consensus segmentation and its mathematical basis, we will report a comprehensive analysis of the IFO 0233 transcriptome elsewhere.

Consensus formation can also be used to aggregate biological replicates data. As an example, we show that the consensus segmentation of the growth curve can be used to determine the growth curve.

The consensus segmentation method incorporates the weight of the reference input segmentation. For example, you can use this feature to weight individual transcriptome data by coverage. In the case of a growth function, the weight can be selected to decrease with the average measurement error, for example quantified as the average deviation from a linear fit. It will also make sense to associate weights with individual segments. Of course, this can be done within the distance of the Boundary Mover's distance. Whether this can also be achieved through potential-based methods, and to what extent the mathematical results of this contribution will remain the same, but this is a question for future research.

We noticed that consensus segmentation is very powerful w.r.t. for the choice of potential on real data, and we observe that the trend tends to be a shorter consensus interval, that is, potential energy $e(z) = z^{\alpha-1}$ on i.i.d. random data, with increasing α. Conceptually, consensus segmentation based on segment comparison is designed to deal with essentially arbitrary heterogeneity along time or genomic coordinates, while break point-centric methods (such as C-KS) require rely on the statistical regularities of real break points. In order to evaluate the utility of different potentials $e(.)$ and dissimilarity measures $D(.,.)$, and compare the use of segment-centered dynamic programming methods for the alternative approach breakpoints centered, it will be necessary to adopt a principled approach to benchmarking consensus segmentation methods.This especially requires the development of a simulator for simulating the relevant segments of different types of basic data characteristics. There is currently no such tool.

CHAPTER 6

Conclusion and Outlook

Conclusion

High-throughput genome assays like microarrays and next-generation sequencing are very efficient tools for studying and interpreting genetic and epigenetic functional elements at the genome-scale [Consortium et al., 2012].

The identification of functional units of the genome usually requires dividing a genome sequence measurements into multiple fragments, where every adjacent fragment have different attributes [Shuai et al., 2014], such as different average values, different gene expression value. Although algorithms have been developed to solve this problem in genomics research, methods with improved accuracy and speed are still needed to effectively solve the existing and emerging genome and epigenome segmentation problems.

We propose in our book with detailed explanation our two new segmentation algorithms: a new "jump size" segmentation method based on decomposition threshold and local optimal differentiation, which can detect significant and meaningful breakpoints in the data to identify segments boundaries. In the second dynamic algorithm, "ConSeg", we get the breakpoint boundary on the size of the consensus segment. The performance of our dynamic algorithms was demonstrated by comparison with pre-existing segmentation methods using both simulated and real datasets. ConSeg provide a powerful and flexible tool for analyzing genomic dataset. Our observations suggest that our proposed segmentation algorithm are effective to identify biologically meaningful regions. The experimental results confirm our theoretical predictions and accord with biologically significant transition points (e.g., cod-ing/noncoding regions, CpG islands, and starting points of genes).

When discussing the "jump size" algorithm here, we propose a conceptually simple scheme for segmenting multi-dimensional data on linearly ordered domains. The algorithm deals with the problem of detecting change-points in the mean of a p-value and local optimal differentiation. The number of changes and their position is unknown. we propose to estimate them with a method based on the Jump-sized decomposition threshold and local optimal differentiation. Using simulated data, we proved that the jump size distribution could be used to determine essential and significant interval boundaries in a data-adaptive manner independent of each data dimension. These segment boundaries can then be combined into multi-dimensional segments.

We also used a simple voting procedure to merge the significant jumps in a suffi-ciently close distance of each data track. Several issues have been identified. We hope that significant improvements can be made in the future: First, a better jump size dis-tribution model will allow for better, statistically reasonable cutoff values-although simple regression heuristics have worked, at least in simulation data is very good. Second, the current rules for combining the segment boundaries of each data track involve a width parameter, which should also be estimated from the data.

Our framework can accommodate different data types, such as genetics, epigenetics, proteomics and transcriptomics data. It is particularly valuable to combine data with different precisions and resolutions. Since the boundaries of each data-track are estimated independently, it is expected that the aggregation process will identify multi-dimensional segmentation with a resolution comparable to the optimal resolu-tion of a single data track.

The consensus of a collection of segmentation can be defined as the segmentation that minimizes the sum of the distances between the consensus and the input one-dimensional segmentation datasets.
In Consensus segmentation "Conseg" work, we have extended and previous general-

ized work by [Mielikäinen et al., 2006, Terzi, 2006] on the segmentation aggregation problem. Conseg showed that for the class of boundedly convex potential functions, including negentropies and powers $z^{1+\alpha}$ with $0 < \alpha \leq 1$, all consensus breakpoints are breakpoints in at least one of the contributing segmentations. Furthermore, we show that for all superadditive potentials, consensus segments cannot be longer than twice the most extended input segment. This bound allows a further reduction of the computational effort.

Consensus segmentations as described in chapter 5 belongs to two major application scenarios: First, Reconciliation of segmentation of multi-dimensional data, comprising, e.g. independent measurements such as biological or technical replicates, or measurements of different quantities, e.g. different histone modifications. Second, Reconciliation of segmentations of the same dataset produced with different similarity measures. In principle, it is also possible to compute the consensus segmentation of different segmentations produced, e.g. with randomized algorithms or different heuristics using the same similarity measures. In the latter scenario, one can also use a dynamic programming segmentation method to select be the best segmentation from the union of the breakpoints of the precomputed by the different heuristics. Such as scheme is e.g. in [Pierre-Jean et al., 2015]. In this manner, one can potentially achieve a substantial performance gain compared to the full dynamic programming segmentation.